Cosmic
Light

Through the higher mind

MARIAN RYAN

Cosmic Light - Through the higher mind

I'd like to dedicate this book to both John and Aimee,
in honour of the journeys we share.
All my love.

Contents

Preface

This book will show you techniques to help you access your core self. It will teach you how to heal through your higher mind and become unattached to past fears and future worries. This will help you ground into, and remain in, the now.

I am an intuitive energy healer, therapist and teacher. Through creative guidance, I've developed a number of energy healing techniques, which I use in my therapies and teachings. I term these Infusion Techniques, as they help you align and integrate the energies of the ego with those of the soul. These have been finely tuned over the years, and I decided to write this book after many clients and students requested for them to be given in written format.

These techniques are very powerful in themselves. They are also powerful when they are combined with other healing modalities, and have very profound results for both client and therapist. They are designed to take you out of the thinking mind, beyond ego, and into your core self within your stream of consciousness, which will enable you to access your genetic, ancestral, karmic, soul group and past/present/future energies.

Healing through the higher self, your true core self, is an extremely powerful way of healing on both a soul and soul group level. It's worth remembering that our soul carries the blueprint of this life and all that's gone before it, as well as the key to unlocking in us our purest highest potential. It's so much easier when life's lessons are learned through the soul than when they are learned through the ego.

I hope that this book helps you heal on the level that's right for you. Over the years, I have seen many souls awaken and find a profound sense of peace and joy, even whilst dealing with some of life's hardest lessons.

I encourage you to develop these techniques as part of your daily self-healing practice. If you find that they work for you, then please recommend this book to others.

Until you become familiar with these techniques, it may be a good idea to ask a friend to read them aloud to you, or you may wish to record yourself reading them aloud and play the recording back when required. Alternatively, they are available for purchase on my website, www.holisticenergy.co.uk.

Matia

Introduction

For me, true healing happens when I can let go and become totally unattached. By this I mean fully release all feelings, thoughts and emotions of any relationship, event or situation that was bothersome, negative, or even traumatic. Letting go of feelings and emotions relating to memories strips them down to a simple recollection. They no longer have any dominance over feelings or thoughts, giving me the freedom to remain unattached, regardless of the trials and tribulations of everyday living, and the challenges they bring.

Science recognises emotional intelligence as a person's ability to be aware of and to monitor their own emotional states, along with those of others, and to find appropriate ways to handle these emotions and grow through and move on from the event that caused them.

Science recognises five parts to emotional intelligence:

1. **Self-awareness:** being aware of and recognising your own internal feelings.

2. **Managing emotions:** using appropriate methods and techniques to manage emotions that are relevant to the situation.

3. **Empathy:** considering and understanding the emotional perspectives of others.

4. **Social skills:** considering your own emotional perspective and the emotional perspectives of others, and using these considerations to develop interpersonal skills.

5. **Motivation:** applying self-control methods to channel emotions toward a goal.

Unless we develop our emotional intelligence, there will be a tendency to misinterpret the emotional signals within our relationships. This is all part of growing up. Whilst a lot of our emotional intelligence is inherent, it is never too late to develop new methods and techniques to help manage emotions.

To express emotions, we need to acknowledge their existence. Simply allowing them to surface into *awareness* will start the healing process. Even old emotions stored deep in the cellular memory can be released once acknowledged. How easy or difficult this process will be is very much dependent on the level of *awareness* we work from.

Emotions

American Neuropharmacologist, Dr Candace Pert (1946 – 2013), identified through her research that we store emotions in the cells (and also in the glands, organs and tissues) of our bodies. She coined the term 'molecules of emotion', and in her book of the same title she stated that 'the brain is a bag of hormones'. Hormones are created in the endocrine glands and act as special chemical messengers, controlling most major bodily functions, from simple basic needs such as hunger to complex systems such as reproduction and even emotions and moods.

As humans, we are naturally designed to discard and renew. Our cells do this without any concentrated effort on our behalf; it is simply done without our awareness. Molecules are atoms bonded together, and they represent the smallest fundamental unit of a chemical compound that can take part in a chemical reaction. Cells continually divide, making more cells for growth and repair in the body. The information needed for this reproduction is held in the nucleus of the cell. Each cell in your body was made from an already existing cell, and these cells store our life experiences - a bit like an autobiography would. The cells hold the blueprint of life. They know our perfection and how to replicate it. Cells are designed with a finite lifespan, and as these die off they are replaced with new ones, with our full autobiography remaining intact. Another important part of a cell is the mitochondrion, which is where food and oxygen combine to make energy. The quality and functioning of the cells impact greatly on the quality and frequencies of the energy we produce.

The food we eat affects the functioning of the brain, just as the cultural, societal, educational, sexual, generational, religious /spiritual and ancestral influences in our life affects our thinking, our beliefs and our mind set.

The mind is the brain in motion. The brain links into every function of our body. The chemical balances within the brain determine the hormones produced. These hormones influence our personality. Our personality is influenced by the astrological alignment at the time of our conception and is further defined by the planetary alignments at the time of our birth. Biology explains how an emotion such as anger can affect the part of the brain that helps us think clearly, and also how it negatively affects the heart.

Dr Pert concluded that the body is the unconscious mind, which can be rephrased as 'mind over matter'. So, if we consciously and/or subconsciously relive past emotional traumas, then part of our subconscious mind can get locked into the emotional rollercoaster ride to destruction.

Now let's take into consideration our higher mind: that wise, unconditionally loving part of us which connects us into our soul essence, Spirit and Divine spark of life, and so into Source.

It is believed that the higher mind influences the brain through the pineal gland. Descartes, known as the 'Father of Modern Philosophy', argued that the pineal gland is moved directly by the human soul. To understand this better, it would help to briefly look at the body's energy systems and how they link into each other.

Everything is energy

Physics recognises that everything is energy, negative or positive. We can neither create nor destroy energy, for it exists in everything. We can, however, transmute energy. Physics states that when a lighter vibration is introduced to a denser vibration the lighter vibration disperses the denser energy, bringing harmony and balance into chaos. Ancient healing and spiritual studies recognise this as transmutation. Scientific research on what's known as 'string theory' suggests that we exist in even smaller particles than those of the atom, and it recognises that we are all interconnected on a multidimensional level.

The Body's Energy Systems

Some of you may be familiar with the energy systems of the human body, others may not, so I shall make a brief introduction to these and request that you carry out further research based on your own needs.

Chinese medicine, acupuncture and reflexology recognise meridians as energy pathways. Meridians transport vital life force energy, also known as Chi. There are 14 main meridians, 12 paired and two single. These link into the major organs and functions of the body. Chakras regulate the flow of the energy that runs through the Meridians.

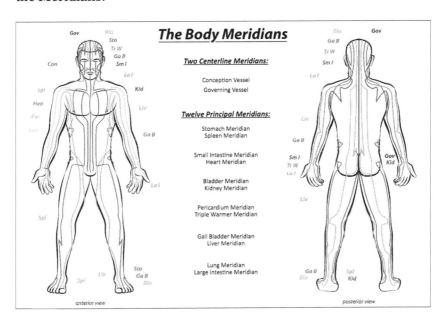

Figure 1: The body's Meridians

The word chakra translates as 'wheel' or 'disk'. There are seven major chakras, which are aligned with the spine and also linked into the endocrine system. These are the base (root), sacral, solar plexus, heart, throat, third eye (brow) and crown. These are considered to be spinning wheels of energy that link the cosmic energy with our human energy field. There are also numerous minor chakras.

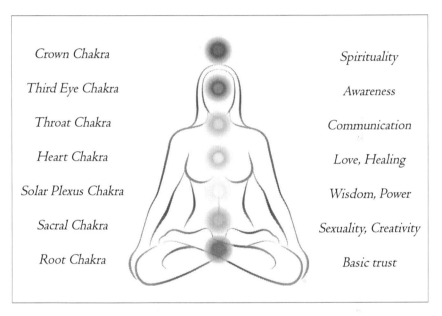

Crown Chakra	Spirituality
Third Eye Chakra	Awareness
Throat Chakra	Communication
Heart Chakra	Love, Healing
Solar Plexus Chakra	Wisdom, Power
Sacral Chakra	Sexuality, Creativity
Root Chakra	Basic trust

Figure 2: The Chakras

The human body, the meridians, the chakras, the organs (and functions of) all interconnect. I like to think of the meridians as motorways, the chakras as roundabouts off the motorways, and the organs and functions as cities, towns and villages off the roundabouts. The meridians are therefore the energy pathways that carry the energy through the body. Any blocks can be likened to a pile-up on the motorway, which in turn creates congestion on the roundabouts; delaying, depleting or, in some cases, severing, the energy supplies to the cities, towns and villages, i.e. the organs, glands and functions of the body. It is, therefore, important that we maintain healthy energy supplies, dealing with any issues and energies as they arise and keeping the flow clear and fluid.

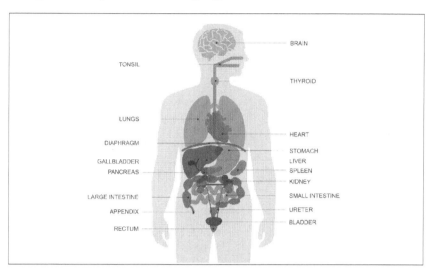

Figure 3: Organs of the body

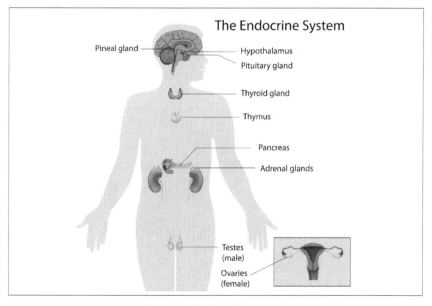

Figure 4: Endocrine system

Stress causes the flow of energy within the body's energy systems to become blocked, especially when long-term stress isn't addressed. This disruption may result in the sense of being 'off sorts', which in turn can lead to physical imbalances and even disease within the body.

All these energy activities and the associated feelings and emotions, combined together, contribute to the conscious, subconscious and super-conscious minds. This is all stored in the memory of our cells.

This book was written with these concepts in mind, and these techniques can be used to support any therapy or any other modality or healing technique. They are intended as empowerment tools for the mind, body, heart and soul. It's important we remember our connection with the earth, and it's equally important that we keep in mind our connection with our soul. We are, after all, 'human' 'beings'. It is the coming together of these two in their purest form that gives us the greatest gift of life.

We carry links to our ancestral line through epigenetics (meaning on top of the gene), which links us to the emotional past of our forefathers, and also through our karmic imprints. The planetary alignments at the time of our conception, and again at our birth, and the ongoing transits of our daily charts contribute to who we are and the energy that makes us unique. We are very fortunate to live on the planet in these wonderful times of healing energy and light.

All we need to do is forgive, let go and open our hearts in love and compassion in remembrance of the fact that we are all at one with Source. The techniques in this book will help you do this.

Whilst there's no necessary order of sequence with these techniques, working through them in the order they appear in the book will help you develop a very strong connection with Mother Earth, thus enabling you to bring more soul essence into this lifetime. Doing these exercises will awaken in you a sense of insight and self-discovery, opening up your intuition and wisdom. They help you find and truly know your true core self. They will also prepare you for a new perspective on life as you explore your inner dimensions. These techniques will help you heal, not just on a soul level, but also on the soul group level, which will impact all of humanity.

Chapter 1

EARTH STAR CHAKRA

The Human Expression of the Energy of the Soul

Your ancestral line is predetermined at your conception. So too is genetic potential and any relevant karmic links. Therefore, your potential starts to form, and your uniqueness and individuality is defined, at your moment and placement of birth. This is where Spirit says to Earth, whilst holding up your birth chart, 'let us both create this *human being*'. The link to this is through the Earth star chakra, which is located in the Earth beneath your feet. The Earth star Chakra holds a blueprint of *who* you are and *what* you're *destined* to be. It's through this blueprint that we emerge *from the Earth* carrying with us energies formed from our genetic, ancestral, karmic, soul group and past life links *to the Earth*. I term these *the family vault*.

At this moment in consciousness, we are very fortunate to be born into a time of great transition and transformation, where human beings are given the option of shedding and discarding karmic energies. We need to redefine our Divine connection to Source, which over thousands of years has been lost and masked in the teachings and dogmas of religion, cultures, traditions, beliefs and hypocrisy, etc. As a result, we as human beings lost the memory of our connection with Source. In order to redefine this connection we need to shed our past through forgiveness, healing, love and light.

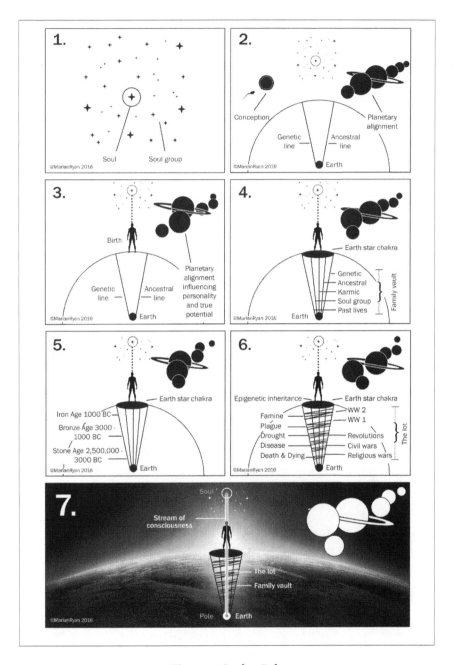

Figure 5: Soul to Pole

The Earth star Chakra supports the physical emergence of the soul purpose into human form. It's where we bring up what we need to *have* in order to support what we need to *be* and *do* in this lifetime. It helps us draw on the strengths, gifts and skills developed in past lives and inherited through the ancestral line. It's these very gifts and attributes that help us to fulfil our soul purpose in line with the Divine plan. It is, therefore, important that we have a very healthy Earth star chakra, and the following techniques are the methods that I've been guided to develop, use and share with others.

Soul to Pole

I understand our soul's relationship with Mother Earth, referenced here as pole, to be as follows:

1. We are a soul forming part of a soul group.

2. The planetary alignment at the time of our conception indicated which ancestral and genetic line we would be born into.

3. The alignment of the planets at the time of our birth finely-tuned this into our personality and true potential. Our birth is where Spirit, whilst holding the blueprint of our life in the form of our birth chart, says to Mother Earth, 'We shall both create a human being.' We are then created as a human form on Earth.

4. The Earth Star Chakra is the link where all this energy comes into form to make the human form of our human being where we are born into the genetic, ancestral, karmic, soul group, past life energies and any other links with Mother Earth. This I've come to term the 'family vault'.

5. If records were available, we would be able to trace our ancestors right back to the first human form on Earth.

6. Then, looking at life up through the ages, we can see the experiences our ancestors would have had in the form of wars, battles, bloodshed, illness, disease, death and dying.

Disasters such as plagues, droughts, famines, etc., leave their imprint on the Earth. Within our connection to the Earth we are linked into every form of human emotion that our forefathers experienced, be it through mental, physical, emotional or spiritual illnesses. Mother Earth holds the energy imprints of all human experiences and reactions - 'the lot' - and these contribute towards our epigenetic inheritance, where we carry the emotional imprint of the generations before us up through the genetic/ancestral/karmic/soul group lines, through the 'family vault'.

7. By stepping into our core self, into our stream of consciousness and connecting with our pure soul essence, we are in a place of non-attachment. From here, we are able to ground into the purest form of Mother Earth. From this place of pure non-attachment, we can access the family vault and heal the lot. Through this, we create for ourselves a Divine link here on Earth, which I've come to term Soul to Pole.

Epigenetics – Inherited Energies

Through the study of epigenetics (meaning on top of the gene), science is now recognising that we inherit a lot of emotional energies from our ancestors. Some studies suggest that this may go back as far as six generations, which in today's terms would indicate that we are still holding the emotional baggage from World War I and World War II, over and above the everyday emotions that our ancestors experienced that were influenced by their familial, social and generational settings. These are all subconsciously feeding into our mindset.

The other factors that influence our energy are the company we keep, the books we read, the music we listen to and the movies we watch. These are all feeding into our subconscious mind, influencing us without us even realising it. Science recognises that every thought produces a chemical in the body, and our hormones are produced in these chemicals, which affect our personalities, behaviours and reactions.

Genetic disorders, or diet-related illnesses, have a major impact on how we feel and think. It is a well-known fact that an overactive thyroid promotes an anxious personality type so a person with this may display impatience and irritability, exaggerated sensitivity to noise, appetite loss, sleep problems and depression. On the other hand, an underactive thyroid promotes a more disinterested personality type. So a person with this condition may display a progressive loss of interest and initiative, a slowing of mental processes resulting in poor memory, lack of energy and vigour, and depression.

Toxic Inheritance

We also carry the heavy metals, chemicals and toxins inherited from our ancestors. These are passed on from generation to generation. A little over 100 years ago, our ancestors readily took highly toxic substances such as mercury as a 'medical cure', ignorant of the damage they were doing in the process. They also used lead, copper, nickel, etc., in their food preparation and storage, and also in their furnishings and paint. They even used it in their make-up. Lead based paint wasn't banned from the UK until the 90s.

We also have the history associated with chemical warfare, such as Agent Orange in the Vitanam war. This had a devastating impact on second generation illness and disease.

Whether these chemicals were ingested or localised through cosmetics, food or chemical warfare, they all contributed to toxic overload in the body, which led to serious illnesses and resulted, in many cases, in neurological and mental health issues. These experiences were stored in the cells of our forefathers, and passed on to the next generation at conception.

While our ancestors can claim ignorance regarding their contribution to the toxic load we've inherited, we can't, as we are well educated today on the effects of toxins and the damage they cause to ourselves, our wildlife and Mother Earth. We can easily clean up the toxic mess we've inherited and break the cycle of toxic overload; this is the legacy we want for future generations. After all, we have access to so much information on how to detox and remain free of toxic overload. We need to look after Mother Earth, for in her purest organic form she provides us with all that we need to sustain us in the healthiest form. For in her healthiest form she provides us with nutrient rich soil, organic fruit and vegetables, and pure water.

Feelings or Thoughts – Which Come First?

Modern science recognises that we have feelings before we have thoughts, whereas the old belief was that we had thoughts that generated feelings. Therefore, it makes sense that we should be very aware of our feelings - yet most people aren't. The reason for this is that we automatically block our feelings when we don't like how we feel. We put barriers up, and we compartmentalise our feelings and emotions, which makes us feel unsafe and insecure. We, therefore, try and regain control and that means externalising everything that's happening, leaving us more and more exposed to the feelings around us, resulting in the need for more and more blocks. Just like illnesses or disorders, this all contributes to our mindset.

Over thousands of years, human beings have lost the natural art of self-protection, self-preservation and honouring their own individuality. This has greatly impacted on their ability to maintain healthy social connections and contribute to the overall impulse of humanity.

In her book, *Molecules of Emotion*, the aforementioned Dr Candace Pert recognised that we store feelings and emotions on a cellular level in the molecules of our being. In her book *My Stroke of Insight*, Dr Jill Bolte Taylor recognises that we are multi-sensory beings and that all these senses merge into our perception of what the present moment looks, sounds, feels, tastes and smells like. Dr David Hamilton, in his book, *Is Your Life Mapped Out?* recognises that we inherit the emotions of the generations before us and that this will include the environments they lived in and the challenges, trials and tribulations they faced. Developmental Biologist, Bruce Lipton, in his book, *The Biology of Belief*, looks at how our beliefs influence our genes. Dr Joe Dispenza, in his book, *Evolve Your Brain*, explains how we process these senses within the framework of the brain that is genetically pre-patterned.

When all of this is compounded into human form and then further abused through misuse of alcohol, drugs, poor diet and a sedentary lifestyle, it further contributes to the blocks and restrictions placed upon the body. In his talk on world peace, the Dalai Lama reminded us that regardless of our consciousness, we are just cells - a biological process in our human form. Science reminds us that proteins are the building blocks of human cells, it's therefore important that we nurture and feed our human form, which impacts on our emotional form, thus influencing our thinking form and contributing towards our spiritual form. We are, after all, 'human' 'beings'.

Are we influenced beyond our control?

Not if we don't want to be. We just need to identify the patterns and the beliefs that influence us and change them. If you want to gain some insight into what emotions are stored where in your body, then Louise Hay's, *You Can Heal Your Life*, and Annette Noontil's, *The Body is The Barometer of the Soul, So Be Your Own Doctor*, are both excellent reference books to help you understand more about the patterns affecting your health, and also what attitude and language changes you need to make in order to break those patterns.

Applying the **Infusion Techniques** listed in this book to your everyday life will help you unattach yourself from negative, limiting patterns and beliefs and enable you make choices in how you want to live your life and the legacy you wish to pass on to the future generations.

The Power of Intention

To achieve all that you do – to think, to plan, to reason, to make decisions, to problem solve, and to manage your emotions – is a major feat of your frontal lobe. In his book, *Evolve Your Brain*, Dr Joe Dispenza describes how the functions of the frontal lobe allow us to learn and grow through our experiences and helps us to work out what we could do differently the next time. His book describes how we have the ability to make a thought become the only thing that is real to us and how the frontal lobe is actively involved in creation.

Andrew Newberg, MD, Professor and Director of Research at Myrna Brind Centre of Integrative Medicine, Thomas Jefferson University and Hospital, is a neuroscientist who studies the relationship between brain function and various mental states. He specialises in a field known as 'neurotheology', which is the neurological study of spiritual and religious experiences and their effects on the brain. His research included taking brain scans of people in meditative states using single-photon emission computed tomography (SPECT) brain imaging technology. His research on the brains of experienced Tibetan Buddhist meditators showed that the frontal lobes were highly active during meditation.

Everything is energy, our thoughts are energy. Once we apply intention to a thought then we amplify its energy. It's important to remember that wherever your focus is that's where your energy is, so whilst doing the following techniques, it is imperative that you focus on what you're doing, and if your mind wanders, which it's likely to do, just bring it back to the technique. Completing these techniques will help you bring your intention, focus and will into full alignment with each other and also into alignment with your soul purpose and the Divine plan.

These are all standalone techniques but they also can be combined. It's totally up to you how you choose to use them.

Technique No. 1 Connecting with your Core Self

This technique is a very simple way of stepping into your light within your own unique stream of consciousness and taking your focus from your external environment and turning inwards and upwards to your soul path and guidance. This will take you and your focus into your core self. Then there will be the grounding into Mother Earth through this energy, which connects your purest form with the purest form of Mother Earth. *These are illustrated in (Figures 6 through to 11, starting on page 29.)*

➢ Imagine yourself to be like a very large tree trunk. (*Figure 6.*)

➢ Carved into this tree trunk is an image of you at every stage or age of your existence, including baby and foetus. (*Figure 7.*)

➢ Imagine a light in your heart centre, which is right in the middle of your chest. (*Figure 8.*)

➢ As you step into this light, you are stepping into your tree trunk and inviting each and every aspect of you to step into your stream of consciousness, asking them to take their focus inwards, onto the inner core self. (*Figure 9.*)

➢ Now imagine that you are standing in a stream of consciousness and above you, pure soul essence is streaming into you. (*Figure 10.*)

➢ From this place, set the intention that you're extending roots - like the roots of a tree - from the soles of your feet and the base of your spine, with an instant connection down to the heartbeat of Mother Earth. (*Figure 11.*)

➢ Imagine the vibration pulsing up through the roots, realigning you with the Earth in your purest form.

> ➤ You are surrounded by every aspect of yourself held in light. In this space, you are safe, you are secure, you are nurtured, you are whole and you are complete.

> ➤ Take as long as this healing needs and, when ready, take your awareness back to your core self.

> ➤ Ground yourself into Mother Earth and give thanks.

From this place of your core self, and through pure intention and connection with the Earth, it is very easy to carry out a number of energy release techniques. These techniques enable very deep healings physically, emotionally, mentally and spiritually. Initially set the intention that you will heal in relation to the following, which I've come to term 'the lot'.

Going forward, you need only set the intention that you will heal 'the lot', and this will be the energy connection your intention will make:

* On all levels and layers of the auric field
* Through all dimensions and realms
* Genetically, epigenetically and ancestrally
* Clearing all karma through the soul and soul group
* Masculine and feminine, past/present/future
* Any others known or unknown to me

Figure 6: Tree

Figure 7: Image carvings

Figure 8: Light in the heart

Figure 9: Stepping into the light

Figure 10: Stream of consciousness

Figure 11: Image roots

Technique No. 2 Grounding Mat – Creating a Vibration Through Intention

Everything in the universe is a vibration. American scientist Dr David Glowacki, a chemical physicist and a Royal Society Research Fellow at the University of Bristol, collaborated with fellow scientists to create the multi-award winning 'danceroom Spectroscopy dS project', which exploits 3D imaging to let people manipulate molecular simulations in real time using their bodies as energy fields. (See www.youtube.com/results?search_query=dance +spectroscopy for a video on this). Dr Glowacki's physics simulation shows the quantum equations of motions, which interpret people as a force field or energy field. (dS) maps how particles vibrate in the field and demonstrates that we all vibrate to our own unique vibration and sound whilst being interconnected in the energy field.

I have found that using a red circular mat, which represents the base chakra and the whole self, and placing four flint rocks from the garden (or just regular stones) onto the edge of it in a square shape representing the Earth, creates a vibration and an intention that the whole self is connected to Mother Earth. By stepping onto this mat you are setting the intention that your whole self is grounding into Mother Earth. This creates a frequency that holds and supports your frequency (as mentioned in the previous chapter, lighter energies disperse denser energies). Some people feel a pulling or pulsing sensation towards the Earth. Each person's response will be individual to them and will vary from session to session.

> ➢ Place a red circular mat on the floor.
> ➢ Place four stones onto the edge of the mat in a square formation, setting the intention that they are connected to each other to form a connection with the frequency of Mother Earth.
> ➢ Step onto the red grounding mat into the frequency of Mother Earth.
> ➢ From this place connect in with your core self (**Technique No. 1**).

> ➤ Set the intention that you're extending roots like the roots of a tree from the soles of your feet and the base of your spine, with an instant connection down to the heartbeat of Mother Earth.
> ➤ Sense this connection with Mother Earth.

The following technique supports this further.

Technique No. 3 Turning on the Taps on the Chakras.

This technique helps you to set the intention that you are 'clearing out' the chakras of old, stagnant energies. It only needs setting up once, then each time you want to work this particular technique, just turn on the 'master tap'.

Figure 12. Tap

➢ Take your awareness to your core self and ground into Mother Earth (taken from **Technique No. 1**).

➢ Take your awareness to the ground beneath your feet, to your Earth star chakra. Imagine a one-way drain allowing all toxic waste from your body to flow down into the core of Earth.

➢ Take your awareness to the soles of your feet and imagine you have a tap on each foot. Turn the taps on and imagine that all fear, vulnerability, insecurity and any other feeling that you identify with are pouring back into the earth, just like the waste from your body.

➢ Take your awareness to your ankles and imagine taps on the inside and outside of your ankles, and also at the top where the foot meets the leg. Turn the taps on and let go of any unsure, unsafe feelings, as well as any other emotions or feelings that come to mind.

➢ Take your awareness to your knees and imagine your kneecaps like the visors on a helmet (you can slide them up). Imagine a tap on both knees, with an outlet to the front and back, turn them on and let go of more fear, vulnerability, insecurity, unsafe feelings, stress, tension, pressure, and any other feelings or emotions that come to mind at this time.

➢ Take your awareness to your base chakra (at the base of the spine) and imagine a tap. Turn it on and let go of all fear, vulnerability, insecurity, unsafe feelings, and any other feelings that come to mind.

➢ Take your awareness to your sacral chakra (two inches below the belly button) and imagine a tap, with an outlet to the front and back. Turn it on. Let go, back to the Earth, all of your feelings and emotions, all of your unmet needs and wants (physical or sexual), all of your guilt, and any other emotions that surface.

➢ Take your awareness to your navel (belly button). Imagine a tap on the navel. Turn it on and let go of all emotional connections with your mother, her mother, and anyone else down the maternal line.

➢ Take your awareness to your solar plexus chakra (two inches above the belly button). Imagine a tap, with an outlet to the front and back, turn it on and let go of the emotions and feelings of other people, the ones that you may have taken on through responsibility or need. Let go of 'the lot', let go of shame, and any other feelings or emotions that surface.

➢ Take your awareness to your heart centre, right in the middle of your chest. Imagine a tap, with an outlet to the front and back, turn it on and let go of all sadness, grief, loss, sorrow, hurts, pains, wounds, scars, jealousy, envy, anger, rage, and any other emotions that surface.

➢ Take your awareness to your higher heart chakra, also known as the thymus chakra. This is located midway between the throat and the heart. Imagine a tap, with an outlet to the front and back, turn it on and let go of anything blocking your true self, your light. Let go of addictions, stagnant energies, toxins, and anything else blocking the flow of energy.

➢ Take your awareness to your throat chakra. Imagine a tap, with an outlet to the front and back, turn it on and let go of secrets, lies, deceits, untruths, harsh words, oaths, allegiances, agreements, promises, vows, and any other feelings that surface.

➢ Take your awareness to your mouth, your eyes, your nasal passages and your ears. Imagine taps on all of these, turn them on and clear your senses of any feelings and emotions that surface.

➢ Take your awareness to your brow chakra (in between your eyebrows). Imagine a tap, with an outlet to the front and back, turn it on and let go illusions, false perceptions, beliefs of limitation, binds, ties, shackles and restrictions, misguided and false teachings, delusions, unhappy memories of people, events, places, and whatever else comes to mind.

➢ Take your awareness to your crown chakra at the top of the head. Imagine a tap, turn it on and let go of whatever is stopping you connecting with your higher self, your higher mind and soul.

➢ Take your awareness to the back of your head, to the part of the brain that speaks to the central nervous system. Imagine a tap, turn it on and let go of whatever is saturating your central nervous system. For instance, any stagnant or sluggish energy.

➢ Take your awareness to both underarms. Imagine taps. Turn them on and set the intention that you are releasing toxins.

➢ Take your awareness to both hands. Imagine taps on both palms. Turn them on and set the intention that you are letting go of anything you are holding onto through fear, through habit, through doubt.

➢ Whilst releasing through all taps, imagine pure light through your stream of consciousness. It's pouring into all chakras from your crown, into your third eye, down into your throat, down into your thymus (higher heart) and heart, down into your solar plexus, down into your sacral, down into your base and down into the Earth beneath your feet. This will be flushing out your system with pure light.

➢ Take as long as this healing needs and, when ready, take your awareness back to your core self.

➢ Ground yourself into Mother Earth and give thanks.

Just get a sense of the energy. If the energy is thick or solid, just imagine the energy of your soul pouring through your crown chakra to the blockage internally, and dissolving it into liquid form. This technique allows you to let go through the taps and replenish through your connection with Mother Earth. All the time you're standing in your core self and in your stream of consciousness with your soul essence pouring through your crown chakra, into your third eye, throat, thymus (higher heart), heart, solar plexus, sacral, base, into the Earth star chakra and down into the genetic, ancestral, karmic, soul group, past/present/future, and any other links. You are clearing back to the Earth whatever needs to go back to the Earth. I've come to term this as 'clearing the family vault'.

To help you understand the term 'family vault', consider the family links here on Earth are both blood and soul connections. These links form the family vault in the genetic, ancestral, karmic, soul group and past life links. The emotional exchanges and experiences these links hold are identified as 'the lot' within the family vault. *Clearing and healing of the family vault are addressed specifically in* **Techniques 6** *and* **9**.

One of my favourite authors is David Furlong. David has written extensively about our connection with Mother Earth. I recommend you read David's book *Healing Your Family Patterns*, as it looks at the energetic links we hold with our ancestors and how our ancestors' experiences helped shape our lives and still continue to affect us today. This book teaches us the importance of clearing energetically what no longer serves us, as doing so can free up and balance the impact these genetic links have on our lives and also the lives of future generations.

Bringing healing into our 'family vaults' helps 'clean up' Mother Earth, as this stagnant negative energy becomes transmuted in light, thereby raising the vibration of Mother Earth.

Master tap

✓ Identify where in your body you would have a master tap.

✓ Imagine a master tap connected to all other taps.

✓ Intend that this master tap turns all other taps on and off.

Tip 1.

✓ When repeating this exercise, just turn on your master tap and all taps will turn on. At the end of the session, imagine you are turning off the master tap, and all taps will turn off. It is just pure intention.

Tip 2.

✓ If doing this before sleeping at night, set the intention for a timer, set to a specific number of minutes, on your master tap. If you fall asleep, the process will complete itself.

Technique No. 4 Surrendering to the Higher Mind

This technique is illustrated in Figures 13 through to 16 below.

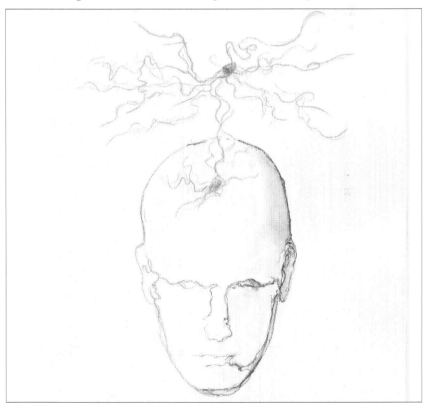

Figure 13. Mind

Figure 14. Conscious, subconscious and super-conscious

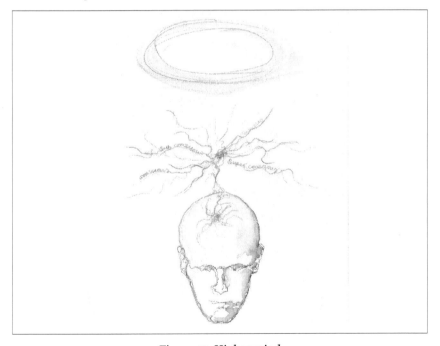

Figure 15. Higher mind

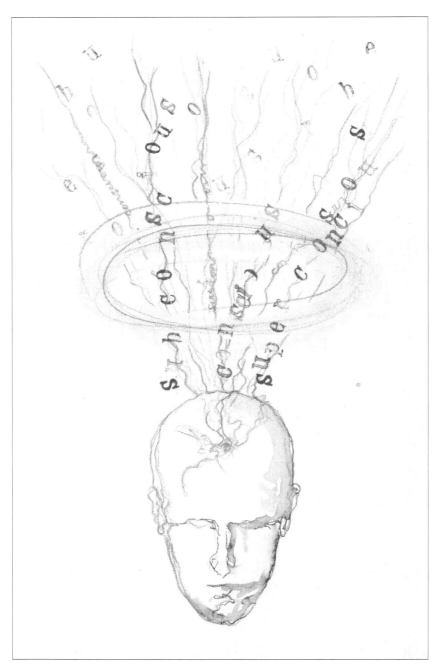

Figure 16. Surrendering to the higher mind

➤ Take your awareness to your core self and ground into Mother Earth (taken from **Technique No. 1**).

➤ Turn your master tap on to release emotions back to the Earth.

➤ Set the intention that you are working with your purest soul and healing 'the lot'.

➤ Take your awareness to your head.

➤ Get a sense of how your brain feels inside your head.

➤ Take your awareness to your mind and get a sense of how that is. (*Figure 13.*)

➤ Take your awareness to your mindset and get a sense of how that is.

➤ Take your awareness to your conscious, subconscious and super-conscious thoughts. (*Figure 14.*)

➤ Take your awareness to your higher mind. You may wish to imagine this as a silver crown hovering above your mindset. (*Figure 15.*)

➤ Observe as you direct your conscious, subconscious and super conscious thoughts up to your higher mind, up through the silver crown. (*Figure 16.*)

➤ In this stream of consciousness and place of non-attachment, you are at one with your pure soul essence and Mother Earth.

➤ Sense these energies pouring into your auric field; they are like a symphony of light.

➤ Observe this light as it penetrates your lower mind and flows down through your body until it connects with your core self.

➤ Sense this wisdom, this soul essence as pure light.

➤ Take as long as this healing needs and, when ready, take your awareness back to your core self.

➤ Ground yourself into Mother Earth and give thanks.

All the time that you are releasing your lower mind up to your higher mind, your taps are releasing all feelings and emotions back to the Earth for transmutation.

For those of you who may have control issues around submitting to your higher mind, consider the fact that the higher mind is still a part of you; it's the pure, all-knowing, wise part of you that knows your past and future. It already knows the outcome of things. For instance, it knows the lessons involved and the thinking behind all of life's experiences. Surrendering to your higher mind is a bit like having your own perfect personal assistant working on your behalf. You need to trust that whatever happens is for your greatest and highest good.

Technique No. 5 Combination Technique

Using the four techniques mentioned above, the Combination Technique allows you to connect with your core self, ground into the purest form of Earth and release emotions back to the Earth for transmutation. You will also surrender conscious, subconscious and super-conscious thoughts to the higher mind. *This **Combination Technique** forms the basis for all other techniques. (These have been illustrated in Figures 6 - 16, earlier in this chapter.)*

➢ Imagine yourself to be like a very large tree trunk.

➢ Carved into this tree trunk is an image of you at every stage or age of your existence, including baby and foetus.

➢ Imagine a light in your heart centre, which is right in the centre of your chest.

➢ As you step into this light, you are stepping into your tree trunk and inviting each and every aspect of you to step into your stream of consciousness, asking them to take their focus inwards, onto the inner core self.

➢ Now imagine that you are standing in your stream of consciousness and above you, pure soul essence is streaming into you.

➢ From this place, set the intention that you're extending roots - like the roots of a tree - from the soles of your feet and the base of your spine, with instant connection down to the heartbeat of Mother Earth.

➢ Imagine the vibration pulsing up through the roots, realigning you with the Earth in your purest form.

➢ Turn on your master tap and set the intention that all negative energies from all chakras pour down to Mother Earth for transmutation.

➢ Take your awareness to your head.

➢ Get a sense of how your brain feels inside your head.

➢ Take your awareness to your mind and get a sense of how it is.

➢ Take your awareness to your mindset and get a sense of how that is.

➢ Take your awareness to your conscious, subconscious and super-conscious thoughts.

➢ Take your awareness to your higher mind. You may wish to imagine this as a silver crown hovering above your mindset.

➢ Observe as you direct your conscious, subconscious and super-conscious thoughts up to your higher mind, up through the silver crown.

➢ In this stream of consciousness and place of non-attachment, you are at one with your pure soul essence and Mother Earth.

➢ Sense these energies pouring into your auric field; they are like a symphony of light.

➢ Observe this light as it penetrates your lower mind and flows down through your body until it connects with your core self.

➢ Sense this wisdom, this soul essence as pure light.

➢ Take as long as this healing needs and, when ready, take your awareness back to your core self.

➢ Ground yourself into Mother Earth and give thanks.

Technique No. 6 Clearing the Family Vault

The Soul to Pole drawing in Figure 5 (page 20) may help with imagery for this technique.

- ➢ Using the **Combined Technique No. 5**, from your core self, ground into Mother Earth, turn your master tap on to release emotions back to the Earth, and surrender thoughts to the higher mind.

- ➢ Set the intention that you are connecting with your pure soul essence and healing 'the lot'.

- ➢ Set the clear intention to clear whatever energy it is you specifically choose to clear.

- ➢ Imagine through your stream of consciousness that you can see down into the family vault, deep into the earth beneath your feet.

- ➢ Ask your soul to take your awareness to whatever energy is relevant and up for healing in relation to your intention at this moment in time.

- ➢ Then set the following intention, stating aloud to the cosmos: *'Under the Laws of Cosmic Light, of All That Is and All That I AM, I intend to step out of this energy and into the energy vibration of forgiveness and light. I ask the over soul to assist my soul in healing and releasing on every level and every layer, 'the lot' so that my soul may know peace. I also open this healing to the whole soul group so that we may know peace and redefine our connection with Source. This is my intention. So it is, it is done, so doth it be.'* (This bridges Spirit with matter.)

- ➢ Then imagine pure soul essence and Divine Light streaming down into the family vault.

- ➢ Imagine it clearing through all stagnant, blocked energies and bringing in light.

➢ Imagine this strengthening your connection with the purest form of Earth.

➢ Take as long as this healing needs and, when ready, take your awareness back to your core self.

➢ Ground yourself into Mother Earth and give thanks.

Technique No. 7 Clearing the Earth Star Chakra

➢ Using the **Combined Technique No. 5**, from your core self, ground into Mother Earth, turn your master tap on to release emotions back to the Earth, and surrender thoughts to the higher mind.

➢ Set the intention that you are connecting with your pure soul essence and healing 'the lot'.

➢ *Focus on the symbol illustrated in Figure 19, on page 133*

➢ Allow the vibration of the symbol to merge with your vibration. (Remember the laws of physics, the lighter vibration cancels out the denser vibration.)

➢ Take your awareness to your energy vibration standing in this vibration.

➢ Intend that your roots are grounded into Mother Earth through this vibration.

➢ Intend that this vibration forms a filter in your Earth star chakra.

➢ State the following intention out loud: *'Under the Laws of Cosmic Light, of All That Is and All That I AM, I intend to bring healing light into my creation, into my existence and into my beingness. I intend to build my foundation on my Divine connection to Source and, in so doing, I intend to tap into my purest potential and the many gifts that I have available to me through my ancestral links and through what I have developed and honed in past and future lives. For this is my soul purpose and these are the gifts that enable me to learn the lessons that my soul needs in this life so that I may be the best I can be. In this space, I connect with Mother Earth, and I draw her energies up through these roots and up into my Earth star chakra. I intend that the vibration of this symbol acts as a filter: cleansing, purifying and strengthening all the energies that come up to make me who I AM. And through the energy of who I AM, I invite the energy of my pure soul essence and the energy of my ego to fully merge, so that I may be a whole and complete human being in light. So it is, it is done, so doth it be.'*

➢ Take your awareness back to your roots, deep into the vibration of the symbol, and into that of Mother Earth.

➢ Set the intention that your earth energies and purest potential are fed up through the roots and through the vibration of the symbol (acting as a filter) into your physical form.

➢ Connect with these energies and sense them in your feet, then up into your ankles, then up into your knees, your thighs, your coccyx and up through your spine, into your sexual organs, your pelvis, your lower abdomen, upper abdomen, kidneys, liver, gallbladder, pancreas, spleen, lungs, heart, blood, bones, muscles and cells. Sense it in your core, your heart and your mind.

➢ Take as long as this healing needs and, when ready, take your awareness back to your core self.

➢ Ground yourself into Mother Earth and give thanks.

Self-Centred Through The Core-Self

This is naturally achieved when using **Technique 1.** When demonstrating this to clients or learners, I normally stand in the centre of my red grounding mat to give a visual image of what it looks like to be self-centred. I also use my dowsing rods to demonstrate the aura size and shape.

When a person uses the core-self technique, they are standing in their stream of consciousness. From this energy, they invite their aspects (the totem pole carvings) to turn inwards and to place their focus and intent on their inner self. In doing so, they become self-centred. This is instantly reflected in their auric field. Their aura takes on a healthy size, which is roughly an arm's length around the body. This gives natural boundaries to the aura and helps the energy feel buoyant and strong. Whilst using the dowsing rods, I ask the person to turn around slowly. As they do this, their aura holds a nice, round, even size and shape, with no distortions or gaps indicated by the movement of the rods. This demonstrates that they are self-centred in their aura.

Aura Sizes and What They Mean

When most clients or learners first come to me, their aura tends to either be too large, too small, or damaged. In some cases, the dowsing rods have indicated an aura wide open to an area of more than 18-feet plus. A large aura might indicate that the person is overstretched, or spreading themselves too thin. Also, the person may be burdened by taking on responsibility for others. When this happens, the person tends to become more focused on external influences, losing touch with their inner self. It also leaves the person depleted of energy and totally drained. However, it can also indicate an intention to control or dominate others.

A small aura, tight into the physical body at the front but distorted and exposed in other areas, tends to indicate fear and insecurity. It's a sign of negative thinking, which results in the need to protect the self. Or it may even be a sign that the person is afraid to be seen, or are holding back because they are unable or unwilling to shine. Creating limitations and restrictions brings emotional stresses very much into physical tensions.

Dowsing Rods

If you have dowsing rods or access to some, ask a friend to measure your aura whilst you step into your core self, and also whilst stepping out of it. Get a sense of what it feels like *in* and *out*. Become familiar with the feeling of being in and sense how complete, whole, safe and strong your aura feels whilst in your core self, or whatever senses you get for yourself.

Point of note: As part of my demonstration, whilst holding the rods, I encourage the client to discuss a particular negative issue. Nine out of 10 times, the rods will indicate that the aura has changed, and they have subconsciously stepped firmly into the negative energy of the issue; they are no longer in their core self. It's easily done, but equally easily remedied. Just step back into your core self, ask your aspects to step in with you and take your focus to the inner self. Then turn the taps on the chakras on, surrender thoughts to the higher mind and observe yourself as you release the emotions that triggered you back to Mother Earth for transmutation. Interestingly, when I asked one client to discuss the issue after the healing, whilst holding the rods, the client remained in their core self. This is because there was no longer an emotion linking them to the event; they were no longer holding the emotional energy in their auric field.

This is addressed further in **Technique No.8**, *which we'll get to shortly.*

When I first did these techniques on myself, I had to keep myself in check and keep putting myself back into my core self. This is such an empowering exercise to do.

The same was demonstrated when I asked a client to focus on a friend's issue. The person came out of their core self and needed to step back in. Once again, once the emotional charge was released it no longer impacted on their aura.

Impacts on the Aura

In our fast-paced world, it's very easy to become embroiled or enmeshed in other people's business, affairs, relationships and energies. This leaves us vulnerable to energy drain and unnecessary worry and stress. Using these techniques allows you to stay unattached to all that's going on around you. Being unattached makes letting go so much easier.

For those of you who might think that being emotionally unattached to other people's dramas leaves you cold and distant, it doesn't. On the contrary, rather than being drawn into the shipwrecks and disasters that render everyone helpless, it means you are more objective and more likely to be strong and supportive when and where you are needed.

With this in mind, some people still have issues with letting go. What I've noticed is that when an event or incident is recalled to mind, some people bring the emotions to the surface. But what they don't realise is that in doing this, they also bring to the surface their block in relation to it. Because they are blocked, they don't feel or sense the emotions and don't realise that they have stepped out of their core self and into the block. Trying to let go through the block is more difficult because the person is now part of the block, whereas when you are in your core self you are unattached and letting go is, therefore, easier. The following technique addresses this.

Technique No. 8 Separating from the Emotion or the Block (The Onesie)

➤ Using the **Combined Technique No. 5**, from your core self, ground into Mother Earth, turn your master tap on to release emotions back to the Earth, and surrender thoughts to the higher mind.

- ➢ Set the intention you are connecting with your purest soul and healing 'the lot'.
- ➢ Recall an event or memory you wish to heal and release.
- ➢ Imagine the emotions of this event or memory have surfaced in your energy as a 'onesie'.
- ➢ Imagine yourself unzipping the onesie.
- ➢ Step out of the onesie and step back into your core self.
- ➢ Imagine placing the onesie on a clothes hanger and place it to the right of you in your aura. You may need to do this a number of times, as there may be many energy layers to the memory.
- ➢ Imagine you are inserting the four symbols (*figures 18-21, on pages 130, 133, 137 and 140*) into the onesie(s).
- ➢ Imagine the energies of the onesie(s) dissolve.

Gratitude and Thanks

As with everything in life, it is very important that we honour and respect the fact that we are multidimensional beings. Whilst we may have forgotten, through the veils of illusion (which by the way are thinning more and more), that we have immense spiritual support, all we have to do, as human beings with free will, is to ask and the help and support will be given. This is done purely through intention. Equally, through intention, we give gratitude and thanks. And in so doing, we set the intention that our aura is aware that the healing is complete and will adjust our energy to the vibrational level required for everyday living, keeping us protected and grounded.

Chapter 2

BASE CHAKRA

Human Awakening into Form

From the moment of conception, our soul's connection with the Earth has already been predetermined. In her book, *Journey of the Soul*, Dr Brenda Davies explains how the etheric body of the foetus enters the mother once the vital essence of the father and mother has united. Thus begins the cosmic formation of a soul purpose, in line with the Divine plan expressed through human form and matter. The ancestral line, the genetics and karmic and soul group energies all lie in wait as potential happening for this soul's journey. This is creation and co-creation with other souls in human form. And so the journey begins. As the foetus develops in the mother's womb, it takes on its destiny, its inheritance and, through epigenetics, the *sins of the forefathers*.

Over millennia, throughout history and time, mankind has lost its spiritual art of knowingness, and the mechanics of existence is very different today to how it was all those generations ago. As human beings, we are designed to manifest on this Earth in line with our soul purpose and the Divine plan. However, through teachings and religious practices that influence our beliefs, actions, feelings, thought processes and everything that contributes to our creation and co-creation with other human beings, the energy patterns that contribute to and create our form have been blinkered and blighted. At birth, planetary alignment strongly influences our potential as human beings. It's as if we finely tune these energy links that make us unique and separate, even though we are all one with humanity and the cosmos. It is these unique identifying traits that contribute to our personalities, our perception of the world, and the reality we manifest. Because we've lost the art and structures of the Spirit-Earth connection, we find ourselves blocked, restricted, negatively influenced and fear-based, and it's these energies that form the foundation of who we have become, living our lives in other people's, i.e., in family and ancestral debris. This leaves us weak and vulnerable, or aggressive and fear-based. But this is just energy and neuroscience and neuroplasticity are helping us to understand that thought creates matter.

The Mind Versus the Brain

The mind influences the brain and not the other way around. Dan Siegel, a professor at the David Geffen School of Medicine at UCLA, explains that 'the mind can use the brain to perceive itself, and the mind can be used to change the brain'. We are only aware of a very small percentage of our thought processes and beliefs because the majority of our thinking is subconscious and influenced by peers, family, religion, society, education systems and organisational structures that we have no intentional part in. Yet we are susceptible to their thinking, and this is the reality we create and so desperately wish to heal. It is my understanding that the very Earth that creates our form contains what I've come to know as the family vault, which holds ancestral feelings, emotions, thoughts, beliefs and experiences, 'the lot', which epigenetics identifies as our inheritance from the generations that went before us. There's much research into this, and I urge you to explore this topic further yourselves. But for the purpose of this book, I make reference to the fact that science is catching up with what Spirit has taught for eternity.

Vibration and Creation

Everything in creation is a vibration. Everything in creation is energy. As Einstein famously said: *"Everything is energy, and that's all there is to it. Match the frequency of the reality you want and you cannot help but get that reality. It can be no other way. This is not philosophy. This is physics."*

We have wonderful scientists, such as Dr Jill Bolte Taylor, who in *My Stroke of Insight* explains how she watched herself have a stroke and observed her entire left brain logic collapse. In so doing, she believes the gift for her was the chance to experience the expansion and creativity of her right brain and, as a neuroanatomist, she fully advocates that people connect with their own right brain and learn the soul connection for themselves. We also have scientists such as Dr David Hamilton, who in *Is Your Life Mapped Out?* encourages the reader to look at the beliefs through which they create and co-create and then separate outmoded beliefs that no longer fit with their growth and expansion.

Discernment

It is important for us as individuals to respect our uniqueness and the understanding that we all have free will to take on board whatever resonates with us at this moment and time in our lives. Whatever feels right will be right for us, regardless of whether it resonates or not with another. This is called discernment. We are fortunate to live in these times of such wonderful planetary shifts. And we are lucky that astrologers such as Kaypacha, Rick Levine and Steve Judd - to name but a few - have been able to explain what's been happening in layman's terms. These shifts contribute to the frequencies and patterns that affect our own unique, individual vibrational pattern and signature that our conception and birth have created for us in this lifetime. Every planetary shift influences the Earth, resulting in vibrational changes to our genetic, ancestral, karmic and soul group energy dynamics.

Vibrational changes and their resulting energy shifts are coming up for every person on this planet at this time. There is no avoiding it, we may block it, we may fear it, but it's preferable that we may work with it. Either way, it will still happen. And yet the truth from my perspective is that part of our soul's purpose is to clear these energies in this lifetime, in alignment with the planetary shifts and changes, altering the very foundation of our being and clearing the debris of the ancestral and karmic lines.

The Fear of Losing Our Identity

To us mere mortals, this may be scary as it impacts on our identity, for example, who we've become, our perceptions, our beliefs and everything we hold dear and our familiarity with the world we've come to know. And yet the true you, the real you, is the expression of your soul essence. Our birth charts contain predetermined potential and possible lessons and skills in life. We have the free will to work with these energies that will help us to flourish and evolve if we so choose. Or, we can continue to do what generations may have done before us, and feed into these energies, cycles and patterns of fear.

It is, therefore, important that we see ourselves, first and foremost, as a soul having a human experience in this life. This is my belief, and if you don't believe in past lives, which I do, you will at least acknowledge that we have an ancestral line. You only need to look through the photo albums of the generations that have gone before you to see the similarities, the traits, the characteristics, the habits, the patterns, the beliefs and the traditions that have been carried from generation to generation. Some of these are positive and beneficial, and some are fear-based - such as religious beliefs of Hell and damnation, or financial beliefs of lack.

Whether you are your own great, great, great grandchild in this life or not is irrelevant. All you need to understand is that we carry threads, cords, links and patterns of energy up through time. These are what influence our subconscious mind, and these are the energies the planetary shifts are bringing to the surface. They provide us with lessons in learning how to tolerate and accept our differences so that we may heal through forgiveness and release.

Are We Grounded or Disconnected from the Earth Today?

The previous chapter included a technique for grounding, not just of grounding into the Earth, but of grounding into your purest potential - this is achieved through the Core Self Technique 1. To be a human being, we need to respect that we are of the Earth and of Spirit coming together. Therefore, we need to have a relationship with Mother Earth so that we may receive the nourishment and nurturing necessary to support our human form, as this is the vehicle for the soul. In this life, good health is achieved through our connection with the Earth. Science now recognises that when we ground, i.e., place our bare feet on the ground, or better still, lie on the ground with our spine and feet in connection with the Earth, it helps us to reconnect to the Earth's subtle, natural, electrical energies. Rubber is a natural insulator and most of the shoes (including the soles) made today are made from rubber or plastic, which block the flow of electrons from the Earth to the body. Most people today are walking around totally disconnected from the Earth. Traditionally, shoes (and soles) were made of leather, which actually helps conduct electrons and therefore maintains a conductive contact between the Earth and your feet.

Basic Needs for Self-Actualisation

The theorist Abraham Maslow (1908-1970) developed the Hierarchy of Needs model in America in the 1940 and 50s. This model is often represented as a pyramid with five levels of needs. Starting with basic needs and working up, they are: physiological, safety, belonging, self-esteem and self-actualisation. Maslow's model is based on the principle that lower level needs must be satisfied before higher-order needs can influence a person's behaviour, only then can they evolve through to their self-actualisation. This theory remains valid today for understanding human motivation, be it for personal development, management training or life coaching.

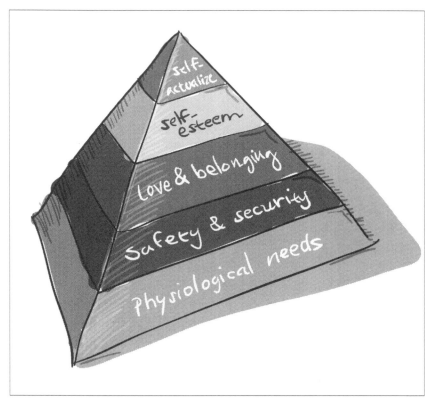

Figure 17: Maslow's Heirarchy of Needs

The Impact of Basic Needs on the Chakras

This is very true of the chakra systems, where the demons of the chakras are known as base/fear, sacral/guilt, solar plexus/shame, heart/sorrow, throat/dishonesty, brow/illusion and crown/attachment. Clearing through our chakras, from base upwards, helps us achieve base/strong(safe), sacral/pleasure (of life), solar plexus/intuitive (will and purpose), heart/open (compassionate), throat/creative (expression), brow/intuitive (wise) and crown/higher (self-connection). This helps us to achieve self-actualisation through the crown chakra. It is, therefore, important that we release back to the Earth everything that came from the Earth. This is mirrored in the natural ability of the human body to shed and discard dead cells, urine, faeces, hair and nails, sweat and tears. This all returns to the Earth where nature knows what to do with it.

Releasing back to Earth all feelings and emotions as simply an energy experience frees us up so that we may have an open mind and be unattached to our experiences. But as we are built on our forefathers' energies, it's important we clear the feelings and emotions we've inherited through the ancestral and genetic line. We can do this through grounding and also through using the technique in the previous chapter, turning on the taps and releasing from the chakras and back to the Earth all feelings and emotions. This enables us to connect in with the purer forms of soul essence and Mother Earth energies. We are exercising our free will to take an experience or event as just energy, and allow it to flow back to the Earth while staying unattached and replacing everything with soul essence and light, further enhancing our deep connection with Mother Earth.

Technique No. 9 Healing the Family Vault

As mentioned in **Technique No 3**, the family vault is what I affectionately term as the genetic, ancestral, karmic, soul group, past/present/future, and any other links we may have to Mother Earth.

- Using the **Combined Technique No. 5**, from your core self, ground into Mother Earth, turn your master tap on to release emotions back to the Earth, and surrender thoughts to the higher mind.

- Set the intention that you are connecting with your pure soul essence and healing 'the lot'.

- Set the intention and your commitment to connecting with Source.

- Take your awareness to the light of the stream of consciousness.

- Imagine this light coming through your crown chakra.

- Imagine this light filling your entire being.

- Imagine it going out through the soles of your feet.

- Imagine it going through your Earth star chakra.

- Now imagine it going down into the family vault, which holds genetic, ancestral, karmic and soul group, past/present/future patterns and forms.

- Set the intention that this healing transmutes all energies that are up for release at this moment in time.

- Imagine this light energy transmuting any negative energies in the family vault.

- Set the intention that any lessons and any beliefs are held in Divine Light so that your soul may be guided through this journey and experience.

- Set the intention that your will is the will of your soul.

- Take as long as this healing needs and, when ready, take your awareness back to your core self.

- Ground yourself into Mother Earth and give thanks.

These techniques help bring you into true alignment with who you really are as a human being. They allow you transmute karmic debt and ancestral lineage and inheritance, transmuting energy links into soul group patterns and forms and bring in healing light so that not just your soul, but the whole soul group benefits.

My journey has highlighted for me that we are responsible for healing ourselves, and all healings are reflected in our contribution to mass energy.

Impacts on Our Physical Matter

The base chakra, from a soul perspective, is the shaping of matter as an expression of the soul purpose. Astrologers such as Alan Oken, looks at astrology from beyond the ego, from the perspective of the soul in line with the soul purpose and formation of matter in this lifetime. Everything is energy. Every thought becomes an energy vibration, and these vibrations create frequencies of energy that stimulate biological and chemical responses within the body through the production of proteins and chemicals. These then become physical matter, influencing who we are, how we think, and what we do.

Our human form is complex yet beautiful in that we are designed to self-heal. Science now confirms that through the constant shedding of cells and cell renewal, we are constantly growing and evolving. Science also understands that our senses send signals to the brain, and it's the amygdala in the brain that recognises our basic survival instinct of fight, freeze or flight. Dr Jill Bolte Taylor has created a wonderful YouTube video (see link below) of the teenage brain, in which she gives a fun and informative explanation of how this all works. (https://www.youtube.com/watch?v=PzT_SBl31-s)

As human beings, we are designed to cope with stress. The body knows what to do and how to do it. But our lifestyles and our advancements have created a lot of white noise and stressful environments, which create unnecessary strains on the systems and functions of the body. In turn, these create toxins and negative chemicals as our brain responds to our feelings.

Our Biological Process

Dr Caroline Leaf, in her book, *Switch on Your Brain*, gives a wonderful, detailed account of the molecular and biochemical processes that *kick in* in response to a thought. There have been numerous medical trials, especially in the field of neuroscience, where brain mapping shows the chemical changes our thoughts create, and it's through these chemicals that our hormones are produced. These chemicals stimulate hormone production and these hormones greatly influence our reactions and behaviours, which influence our personality traits. Science has also identified how having positive thoughts, such as during mindfulness, creates positive chemicals. These positive chemicals influence the hormones, which in turn influence our reactions, behaviours and personality traits. So basically speaking, it's never too late to recreate *what* you want in life or *how* or *who* you want to be.

Influential factors – environmental and spiritual

As mentioned earlier in this book, our energy is influenced via inherited energies feeding up through the Earth creating us in form. We also have environmental, spiritual, social, generational and cultural influences, to name but a few. And once again, this is where free will plays a major role in who you are and the reality you create. It is my belief that our soul chooses the lessons for this life, and in so doing at the time of conception, and in particular at birth, Mother Earth creates the human form as an expression of the needs of the soul.

Our spiritual advancement is helping us to realise that we need to revert back to our spiritual traditions and the practices of our connection with the Earth. This is so that we may fully function and take these experiences within the life that we have chosen and created. And, through our own willpower and spiritual insightfulness, we may evolve and self-actualise our soul purpose in line with the Divine plan.

It is, therefore, crucial that our base chakra, Earth star chakra and family vault receive the healing from Mother Earth and soul essence. In turn, parents, siblings, relatives and friends (or whoever benefits through your soul group) will all grow and evolve through the self-healing and self-actualisation of your soul journey. Healing your soul aspects, down through your whole soul existence, opens the healing pathway for your whole soul group. Healing through your soul strengthens your connection with Mother Earth and allows more soul expression in this lifetime. This is what we should be teaching our children, and these are the examples we should lead by in every relationship and interaction in our life.

Inner Peace

The Dalai Lama XIV famously stated: 'I believe all suffering is caused by ignorance. People inflict pain on others in the selfish pursuit of their happiness or satisfaction. Yet true happiness comes from a sense of inner peace and contentment, which in turn must be achieved through the cultivation of altruism, of love and compassion and elimination of ignorance, selfishness and greed.'

As human beings, we need to learn to work with Mother Earth. We come from the Earth and upon our death, we will return to her. She stores the impressions and imprints of our past, present and potential. Mother Earth is depleted of her natural minerals. If you look at parts of South Africa, where Mother Earth's natural mineral resources have been extracted, leaving the land totally depleted, is it a coincidence that the people are experiencing exceptionally high levels of auto-immune conditions?

Scientists in the 30s and 40s warned us that the soil was depleted and that something needed to be done to rectify it. Since then food manufacturers and pharmaceutical companies have further exploited the Earth through the use of harsh chemicals and the introduction of GM foods, depleting mineral flow even more. Minerals are the core of our being. Without minerals, our bodies are unable to absorb vitamins. Iron, for instance, is a typical example of this. Taking Ferrum Phos. tissue salt remedy helps the body to absorb and use the mineral effectively in the absorption of iron.

Once the body's mineral salts are replenished, then it can repair itself through nutrition. Good quality organic foods are best, but even then the quality of the soil impacts greatly on the quality of the food. It's important that we support our physical body. In her book, *Tissue Salts For Healthy Living*, Margaret Roberts gives an in-depth account of the importance of mineral support in the body's development, growth and ageing processes.

We are currently at a vibrational level where we can process energies from our higher soul dimensions, bringing them into Earth form in 4th and 5th-dimensional energies and processing Earth experiences at a much higher vibrational rate, therefore supporting our soul's evolution.

Chapter 3

SACRAL CHAKRA

Soul Brothers and Sisters are Companions Along our Path to Wisdom

From my own personal experiences and my inner guidance, I find the following technique helps my soul to fully experience whatever it needs to experience from the events and occurrences in my life. This highlights to me that we are but the vehicle for the soul and that once we start experiencing life on a soul level, then lessons become easier and healing is quicker and letting go is so smooth.

Science identifies that the human brain matures around the age of 25. So when we're little, our brain isn't able to comprehend our relationship with the soul, nor can it understand how we carry into this life our spiritual practices and any fears and blocks that we've had in past lives, along with the ancestral and karmic baggage we inherited at birth. All of these combined provide us with life's lessons. These lessons are in line with the soul purpose and Divine plan. It is, therefore, important that as adults we reflect back on our inner child's pains, hurts and lessons, and heal via the soul.

Technique No. 10 – Experiencing Hurts and Pains Through the Soul

> Using the **Combined Technique No. 5**, from your core self,

ground into Mother Earth, turn your master tap on to release emotions back to the Earth, and surrender thoughts to the higher mind.

➢ Set the intention that you are connecting with your pure soul essence and healing 'the lot'.

➢ Imagine yourself holding your heart, or your heart centre, in both hands.

➢ Imagine yourself raising your hands up to your soul.

➢ Say out loud the following intention to your soul: *'Under the Laws of Cosmic Light, of All That Is and All That I AM, I ask Dear Soul that you fully experience these hurts and pains so that I may forgive and let go with ease. I also ask that my higher mind helps me to find peace of mind in my acceptance, tolerance and forgiveness of the past and all parties involved. So it is, it is done, so doth it be.'*

➢ Get a sense of your higher mind downloading patterns of peace into your lower mind.

➢ Get a sense of your soul's release.

➢ Imagine cosmic light pouring into your existence.

➢ Take as long as this healing needs and, when ready, take your awareness back to your core self.

➢ Ground yourself into Mother Earth and give thanks.

For many people, the sacral chakra is associated with sexual desire and it's linked in with the sexual organs and our ability to receive pleasure. It's important to remember that this is also where we store our needs and desires, and sometimes that may be something as simple as being picked for the football team at the age of 10, asked to the prom at 16 or given a hug when we need one. These are the inner child aspects that we need to heal. In doing so, we heal our relationships. There has been much research into the social development of children and how we learn from our nearest and dearest. We develop our negotiating skills and our confidence through interactions and exchanges with our siblings, classmates, neighbours and friends.

Through these relationships our soul gains most of its experiences, and yet our innocence and naivety prevent us from seeing the enormous potential for soul growth and development. Through our fears and insecurities, we develop these experiences into personality flaws, and we own them for life. Regardless of how debilitating they are, or cumbersome they become, we're always reluctant to let them go. Instead, we believe that they are at the core of who we are. We fail to realise that what we're clinging to is just familiarity.

Inner Child

A lovely exercise to do is to connect with your inner child and get to know her or him. We all have one, each and every one of us. You too have a part of you that wishes to heal. And no matter how happy our childhood, or how safe and secure we felt growing up, there is still a child within who is carrying its own hurts, pains and naive perception of the world. And whether that world is seen through the eyes of fear, shame, guilt, blame, injustice or inadequacy, we need to remember the enormous influence the subconscious mind has on how we feel. It influences how we react to life's events.

As mentioned before, science now understands through the study of epigenetics that we're born with feelings, emotions, beliefs and thoughts inherited through the experiences of our forefathers. So whilst life today may be idyllic, we're still carrying wounds that need healing. And involving your inner child, who knows all your secrets, failings and flaws (be they yours or others, or gained through inheritance or peer pressure) gives you the opportunity via your soul to heal and release. For some people, it's inconceivable that we may carry an inability to forgive or hold resentment through the ancestral line, but it's all learnt behaviour and anything you've trained your mind to do can be untrained. The following technique is a beautiful way to connect with the child within and introduce that aspect of you to your soul, and it's this relationship that brings about the deepest, most profound healings. It truly can be the start of a very deep connection with your soul.

Technique No. 11 Inner Child/Soul Union

➢ Using the **Combined Technique No. 5**, from your core self, ground into Mother Earth, turn your master tap on to release emotions back to the Earth, and surrender thoughts to the higher mind.

➢ Set the intention that you are connecting with your pure soul essence and healing 'the lot'.

➢ Call upon Mother Earth to hold and support your human form during this technique.

➢ Imagine yourself grounding and connecting through roots into the safety, security and nurturing provision that Mother Earth is able to give you.

➢ From this place, imagine in your heart centre a beautiful garden or an image of your favourite location.

➢ Take your awareness to the pure, high vibration this creates in you.

➢ Invite to this place that little inner child within you that wants to step forward. Reassure them that they are in a very safe and secure place within you and that you are in your purest form.

➢ Ask your soul to hold this little you in the highest, purest vibration.

➢ Ask your soul to experience through this little one whatever soul lesson you blocked at this age.

➢ Sit with your little one for a few moments in whatever way feels comfortable for you, whether you imagine it through embrace, holding hands, or just being in the company of your little one. Just do whatever feels natural for you and them.

➤ Take as long as this healing needs and, when ready, take your awareness back to your core self.

➤ Ground yourself into Mother Earth and give thanks.

Sometimes it helps to write out some questions beforehand that you may want to ask your little inner child. But once you've formed a relationship and reconnected with that bond, the conversation will flow with greater ease as you grow in trust and feel confident with your newfound connection with your inner self.

I like to ask my inner child what they would like me to do to help them feel happy. And the reply might be as simple as colouring in, reading, playing, dancing or baking. And I make the effort to do it. I'd like you to do the same. Promise yourself that when you do, you'll connect with your inner child so that you both may share the pleasure and the happiness that the experience brings. Remember to always honour the promises you make to your inner child, and never promise anything that you won't or can't follow through on. They're far more resilient than we give them credit for. What you have to remember is that whatever your experiences in life, they've survived, they got you through them. And what you need to help them do is let go of the emotional charge so that they may move beyond the experiences.

The Energetic Importance of Healing Your Past

As humans, it's in our nature to want to help others. We feel great joy when we find a purpose in life, and if it's your nature to want to help or heal, it's very easy to overlook your own needs in favour of someone else's. Sometimes helping others means that we don't have to look at our own wounds, and sometimes it eases our own pain. But all of this is short-lived, especially if we move from person to person (be it a client or a friend), enabling them to heal and let go but never quite achieving it for ourselves. And yet with our greater understanding of the body-mind connection, especially through studies such as dance Spectroscopy with Dr David Glowacki, we understand how our energies merge with one another.

We now realise that self-healing impacts greatly on those around us. When we heal and clear karmic energies, this means we no longer need to *play it out* within our relationships or our soul group. So I urge you to take it upon yourself to make the commitment to your soul that you will heal your *past*. In doing so, you will create a peaceful and calm *now*, which in turn will influence your *future*. When this is done through the soul expression, it will help you to remain unattached to the dense, heavy emotional debris of those around you and instead form your connections on a much higher frequency of the soul. We are, after all, multidimensional beings and connect on many, many levels, far beyond our human comprehension.

The following technique is a beautiful way to combine soul and inner child healing.

Technique No. 12 Vibrational Symphony Between Soul and Mother Earth

- ➢ Using the **Combined Technique No. 5**, from your core self, ground into Mother Earth, turn your master tap on to release emotions back to the Earth, and surrender thoughts to the higher mind.

- ➢ Set the intention that you are connecting with your pure soul essence and healing 'the lot'.

- ➢ Standing in this place, imagine your connection becoming deeper and deeper within this beautiful stream of consciousness inside yourself.

- ➢ Imagine yourself stepping deeper and deeper into that light.

- ➢ Invite your soul and Mother Earth energies to join you,

creating a beautiful symphony of vibration.

➢ Imagine yourself being held in this vibration.

➢ Connect with your little inner child by inviting them forward to sit with you in this energy vibration in whatever way feels right and comfortable for them.

➢ Reassure your inner child with whatever words come to mind. You may say things such as: 'Thank you for helping me here today'/'You are safe and secure'/'I love, accept and respect you'/'I'm very proud of you.'

➢ Imagine yourself being held in the beautiful symphony of vibration that your soul and Mother Earth create.

➢ Take as long as this healing needs and, when ready, take your awareness back to your core self.

➢ Ground yourself into Mother Earth and give thanks.

It might be that this is as far as your inner child will be willing to go with the healing, and respect that. If, however, your inner child is willing to help you to heal then continue as follows...

Technique No. 13 Soul and Inner Child Healing

Continued from **Technique No. 12** *above.*

➢ From this beautiful frequency of light, say to your inner child some words, such as: 'I love you and fully respect how you feel and what you think. I'm the adult now, and it's up to me to make sure we are safe and feel loved. All these old feelings that we carry have grown and multiplied, and they no longer fit in with our higher frequencies. Therefore, we need to let them go in exchange for higher vibrational feelings. I need your help in letting go. I ask that we hold our heart in our hands and lift it up to our soul. We ask our soul to experience these feelings in whatever way is necessary that we may grow on every level and be open to forgiving, healing and letting go, regardless of the memories, the comprehension and the perceptions of us and those around us that may have influenced these feelings at that time. And I ask you, little one, to allow our soul access, as I hold you in light and show you that it's safe and okay to release these back to the Earth. And I ask you, little one, to trust. Trust our soul and our connection with the Earth so that we may be free. And I ask this for our greatest and highest good, and the greatest and highest good of all concerned. So it is, it is done, so forever doth it be.'

➢ Sit with your little one in the vibrational symphony created between the energies of you, your soul and Mother Earth.

➢ Take as long as this healing needs and, when ready, take your awareness back to your core self.

➢ Ground yourself into Mother Earth and give thanks.

Saying something three times sets the intention with the universe that your intention has been activated, and you accept wholeheartedly that it is done. It bridges Spirit and matter. When working in this way, you will find that memories and feelings of the past may come to light. This is your soul's way of bringing to your awareness, via your inner knowing, of what needs healing so that you may grow on a soul level in line with your soul purpose and the Divine plan.

Embracing the Whole Self

You may wish to combine a number of different techniques at any given time. Whatever combination you choose, it is important that you are grounded into Mother Earth, releasing through the master tap technique and encouraging your chakras to fully release back to the Earth, further supporting your healing intention and deepening your connection with the Earth through heartfelt and soul-felt release. I always like to thank my inner child. This shows respect, gratitude and trust, and it also shows my inner child that I believe in her and that I have great hope for our future. It helps me to fully embrace my whole self, allowing me to be whole and complete. Healing this way is what true self-control is. Society has taught us that self-control is to control our environment. As adults, we find ourselves saturated with everything we took on through attempts at self-control. But once on a healing journey, especially one of this nature - deep soul and inner child - we realise the importance of un-attachment and release.

A lovely and creative way to use these techniques is to practise them in line with the exercises in Louise Hay's book, *Mirror Work*. Making eye contact with yourself through a mirror helps you to form deep connections with all aspects of yourself.

We Are Designed to Eliminate

If we look at all the systems of elimination in the body that occur naturally to support our functioning, we see that everything that's humanly made returns to the Earth. And that's where our feelings, emotions and thoughts need to go. Forgive and let go with ease, don't gather and store.

We're very fortunate that there is so much information available through the internet and via the vast array of books that are readily available and easily accessible through numerous means of communication. These offer guidance and advice on every imaginable topic to support us physically, emotionally, mentally and spiritually. It's up to each individual to discern for themselves what is right for them at this moment in time on their path. For we are all different, and we all have our own soul purpose and role to play in the Divine plan. We are, after all, independent beings with interdependent energies existing on multidimensional levels.

Healing the Soul is Our Path to Wisdom

As mentioned previously, our connection with the Earth, our genes, our karma and our personality traits are unique, and when combined with our needs and desires at any given moment in life, they influence our relationships with ourselves and with others. Yet the very simple intention of involving our soul in all these needs and desires creates a very different form because working via the soul is our path to wisdom. Through our soul essence, we can bring this wisdom to our needs and desires and into our relationships, giving us greater insight into the lessons and opportunities for growth that these exchanges give us.

When we bring soul wisdom into our relationships, we exercise more tolerance and more acceptance of our diverse traits and perceptions. It helps us show more compassion, more forgiveness and it enables us the wonderful opportunity to not take personally the events and circumstances that happen in the lives of others. This allows us to remain unattached and avoid becoming embroiled or enmeshed in the life lessons of other people. This wisdom permits us to have exchanges with people instead of enmeshment, allowing us to experience, grow, release, let go and move on with grace and ease through the numerous lessons our soul journey takes.

Soul contracts

When we learn to look at our brothers and sisters on a soul level and respect the contracts and exchanges that our souls have undertaken in this lifetime, and when we respect life on these levels, it brings this path of wisdom into our wider family unit. It opens our heart in such a profound way that it enables wisdom and dissolves fear so that our souls may always find peace in all of our exchanges. We each have one soul, and it's my belief that we have many, many lives.

Sometimes we fail to learn our soul's lessons and we carry them from lifetime to lifetime. Whilst these lessons may appear burdensome and difficult, once we fulfil that contract on a soul level that's it, we can move onto the next lesson and fully complete cycles in this lifetime, along with patterns. This finality travels down through the ancestral line, clearing the way for the generations to come.

Any future lives we may have down this ancestral line will be held in wisdom and soul essence, and this brings about very deep profound healings for all concerned. When I do my personal healings, I like to take my awareness from my stream of consciousness and allow soul essence to pour through into my ancestral line, genetic line, the karmic line and the soul group, and into what I affectionately term the 'family vault'. This brings in healing light and sets the intention that whatever I've healed via my inner child and via my heart and my soul is healed on every level; every layer, every dimension and realm; physically, emotionally, mentally, spiritually, past/present/future, masculine and feminine, and any others known to me or unknown to me. I term all of this 'the lot'. I like to set the intention with all healings that they are completed through the term 'the lot'.

Technique No. 14 Healing the Inner Abode

It's my belief that we are literally standing in the footsteps of our forefathers, and that any signatures from the ancestral line and patterns have left their imprint in every step throughout history and time. Resulting in the shared ideas, beliefs, patterns and attitudes. And this is the very energy that impacts on our signature. This is the energy that influences our inner child. I feel very guided to set the intention that my inner child's abode is healed and is a safe, nurturing and loving place in which my inner child resides.

> Using the **Combined Technique No. 5**, from your core self, ground into Mother Earth, turn your master tap on to release emotions back to the Earth, and surrender thoughts to the higher mind.

> Set the intention that you are connecting with your purest soul essence and healing 'the lot'.

- ➢ Become aware of your stream of consciousness.
- ➢ In that pure human form, ask your soul to fill you with light and hold you in the purest potential as a human being, knowing that you are safe.
- ➢ From this place, and within that stream of consciousness, set the intention that you can sense your father's stream of consciousness.
- ➢ Imagine that you can sense beyond that into mass consciousness.
- ➢ Take your awareness to where your father's stream of consciousness connects into yours.
- ➢ Set the intention with your inner child that you hold in your heart all of the feelings this stream of consciousness triggers in you.
- ➢ Imagine that you are holding your heart up to your soul.
- ➢ State out loud: *'Under the Laws of Cosmic Light, of all That Is and All That I AM, I ask, dear soul, that you experience these energies, the lot, and that you help me open my heart centre. And, through my pure connection with Mother Earth, help me to forgive, heal and release back to the Earth so that I may know peace. So it is, it is done, so forever doth it be.'*
- ➢ Imagine your heart being healed as your soul releases back to the Earth.
- ➢ Imagine pure cosmic light pouring into your mind, heart, core and right into your inner abode.
- ➢ Imagine strong, safe, confident, pure energy cocooning your inner abode.
- ➢ Get a sense of what this feels like and fully embrace it.
- ➢ Take as long as this healing needs and, when ready, take your awareness back to your core self.
- ➢ Ground yourself into Mother Earth and give thanks.

Repeat this technique to address the energy connection through your mother's stream of consciousness.

Technique No. 15 Healing Energy Links with Parents

As we walk in the energy footsteps of our parents and grandparents, we naturally tap into these energies and take them on as our own. These may take the form of specific personality traits our soul wishes to experience in this life, or they may be a result of learned behaviours our ego fully identifies with.

I recommend that you complete this technique with each parent.

➢ Using the **Combined Technique No. 5**, from your core self, ground into Mother Earth, turn your master tap on to release emotions back to the Earth, and surrender thoughts to the higher mind.

➢ Set the intention that you are connecting with your purest soul essence and healing 'the lot'.

➢ Connect with your inner child in the vibrational symphony between soul and Mother Earth (**Technique Nos. 12** and **13** above).

➢ In this space, set the intention with your inner child that you are open to receiving the guidance and wisdom of your soul.

➢ Imagine the compassion and acceptance of the soul journey you took on with your parent (regardless of life's circumstances), and the experiences and events you shared.

➢ Imagine yourselves as souls fulfilling your soul's purpose in line with the Divine plan, and remember that these exchanges up to now were via your egos. Understand that you are now working soul to soul.

➢ Take your awareness to the particular energy link with this parent, be it in the form of a belief, an attitude, a habit or a trait.

➢ Set the intention that you are reclaiming and returning any energy exchanges with this parent that created, or contributed to, the energy link by saying out loud: *'Under the Laws of Cosmic Light, of All That Is and All That I AM, I reclaim my energy and my power. Any energy or power I took from you, I return to you. Any energy or power you took from me I reclaim. I do this for the greatest and highest good of all concerned. So it is, it is done, so doth it be.'*

➤ Imagine the guidance and wisdom of your soul being downloaded through your higher mind into your lower mind.

➤ Realise that the higher frequencies this brings enables you to fully surrender everything of human form back to the Earth, and everything of Spirit to Source.

➤ Imagine yourself bringing through a higher frequency of healing light.

➤ Take as long as this healing needs and, when ready, take your awareness back to your core self.

➤ Ground yourself into Mother Earth and give thanks.

This can also be completed for step parents, foster parents and adoptive parents, etc.

Endocrine System

The endocrine system is composed of several glands. Each gland has its own role to play in the body, but the actions overlap, affecting one another as each gland works both alone and together to coordinate the body's functions. In a healthy person, the glands function well and with little effort as each gland produces and secretes hormones that excite or inhibit various tissues in relation to metabolism, growth and reproduction. Stress, however, creates havoc in the endocrine system. This stress may be in the form of physical stress, i.e., a broken bone, excess heat, cold, etc., emotional stress, e.g., anger, fear, rage, etc., chemical stress, e.g., alcohol, sugar, caffeine, artificial flavourings, food colouring, GM foods, etc., electromagnetic stress, e.g., from mobile phones, laptops and tablets, etc.

A healthy endocrine system supports the link between the human form and the soul. The philosopher Plato believed the thymus was part of the soul, expressing itself as pride, shame and indignation. He saw it as an internal warrior aspect of human form seeking validation in life. He believed the thymus offered moral autonomy, and that without it, man would be nothing but an intelligent animal with a brain and control of physical activities.

As mentioned in the introduction, Descartes believed the pineal gland is moved directly by the soul.

I like to end all healings with the intention that in my stream of consciousness my endocrine system is balanced and in full alignment with my soul.

Technique No. 16 Rebalancing the Endocrine System and Supporting Organs

> Using the **Combined Technique No. 5**, from your core self, ground into Mother Earth, turn your master tap on to release emotions back to the Earth, and surrender thoughts to the higher mind.

> Set the intention that you are connecting with your pure soul essence and healing 'the lot'.

> Imagine the light of your pure soul essence bringing through cosmic light.

> Imagine this as a laser beam of pure, cosmic light.

> Imagine the laser penetrating each gland and supporting organ, as follows, refer to *Figure 4: Endocrine System on page 16*.

o Pituitary

o Pineal

- o Hypothalamus
- o Thyroid
- o Parathyroid
- o Thymus
- o Adrenals
- o Kidneys
- o Pancreas
- o Ovaries/testes
- o Glands in the groin

➢ Imagine the laser balancing and harmonising each gland.

➢ Imagine the stress being transmuted into light.

➢ Ground this beam of light down into the family vault.

➢ Create a sense of feeling very strong and very safe in this creative expression.

➢ Celebrate your uniqueness, your oneness with your soul and allow yourself to be a pure, creative expression of pure soul essence.

➢ Now simply be present in the moment.

➢ Take as long as this healing needs and, when ready, take your awareness back to your core self.

➢ Ground yourself into Mother Earth and give thanks.

Creativity

Creative expression is our God-given right, and each person will have their preferred or chosen modalities in which to articulate their needs, desires and their creative outlet for their soul's expression. We grow through trial and error, and we intuitively know what feels right for us. The simple act of honouring this, regardless of other people's perceptions and projections, gives us license and freedom to shine in the world and be who we truly are. The greatest gift we can give ourselves (and others) is to honour this creativity and allow ourselves the freedom of expression without limitation or restricting beliefs.

For your soul to fully express itself in its most creative form, you need to have an open heart of compassion, love and light. To achieve this, it may be necessary to bring healing into the ancestral line, genetic, karmic, soul group, past lives and past/present/future lives. And if you've never believed in past lives, you only need to look at the patterns of behaviour and beliefs along the ancestral line projected from generation to generation. See how they block, limit and restrict on every level, hindering all opportunities for creative expression.

Chapter 4

SOLAR PLEXUS

Free Will Wisely Used Helps us Express our Differences With Each Other

From the perspective of energy healing, our own intake and output of energy have a great impact on our interactions and exchanges with those closest to us. We have what's known as free will, and yet we have a destiny. There are numerous thoughts and teachings on this subject, and I urge you to discern for yourself what works for you. It is, however, my understanding that our free will is basically the choices we make in fulfilling our destiny. It's the *how* we go about doing the *what* we need to do. As mentioned in previous chapters, our birth chart influences our personality, so, whilst some souls may decide on a life where they are forceful characters that desire power and status, other souls might be more introverted, prefer the quieter life and may even be reclusive. It's these differences that make us unique. They also make our exchanges with others so varied and diverse.

The solar plexus is our powerhouse. It should be a one-piece, gilded picture frame of who we are now. Yet most of us end up with a thousand-piece jigsaw puzzle, with most of the boundary pieces missing and unidentifiable because we lose our identity by giving away our energy and power to others.

Self-empowerment

Self-empowerment is very different to how the world perceives *being powerful*, and these differences are important to note, as true self-empowerment comes from within. The **Core Self Technique** in Chapter 1 will help you to step into your core, your true self, and it's from this place that you should heal and reclaim your power and sense of self. It is my understanding that we are all one on a soul level. We are all connected energetically on a soul level. And yet, our relationships with others are mainly carried out through our ego and through fear, lack, doubt, guilt, shame and blame.

The demon of the solar plexus is shame, and as children, we are made to feel this emotion in response to our behaviours. Adults instil shame in children as a way of controlling them and achieving desired responses, behaviour and attitudes. Through shame, we learn to doubt ourselves and blame others. Shame generates cycles of perpetually projecting negative energy, either onto ourselves or others and into past events. It is these feelings and influencing thoughts that cause us to develop habits and formulate beliefs. We then carry these into our adult lives and in turn project them onto those around us, especially our own children. This continues down through the ancestral line and feeds into the epigenetics.

Enmeshment

We are multidimensional beings who have chosen this life in this lifetime. But we are also born into cultural and generational beliefs and energies. The planets influence us through all our developmental stages, from foetus to toddler, right through to middle and old age. Because we have learned to hold onto our pains and experiences, these become deeply rooted in every aspect of our being. For some people, these influences may have resulted in growth and expansion, for others, it may contribute towards blocks and fear. To become empowered, we need to heal these blocks and fears.

Every experience we have in life impacts on our auric field. Scientists such as Dr Jill Bolte Taylor and Dr Joe Dispenza teach that we have feelings first followed by thoughts, and not the other way round (as was believed in the past). So when we hold onto these feelings and fuel them with our thoughts, we create more energy - more of the same - and we fill our own auric field with toxic energies.

For those of us who are sensitive, we feel other people's feelings, especially so if their emotions become heightened or escalated. If this is continuous over time, we become enmeshed in the other person's energy, blurring our boundaries. Before long, we are no longer able to distinguish our emotions from theirs. This is very unhealthy and can be quite draining.

Hidden Aspects

As adults, we may sometimes wish to change a habit or a pattern and find it difficult to do so, as we meet obstacle after obstacle. Yet finding and working with the very aspect of us that is holding that energy and fuelling it through our subconscious will enable us to heal to the core. To do this, the following technique is a method of finding a safe, neutral, secure place in which to meet the hidden aspects of ourselves. It will help us to access aspects of ourselves for each year of our existence, plus one for our baby year and one for our foetal growth.

It is important to note that when we have traumatic events, or events that as an adult may not seem traumatic or distressing, these may be so to a child, our inner child. We tend to lock these aspects of ourselves into that moment in time. These aspects are constantly reliving those heightened emotions, sometimes conscious, other times subconscious. Therefore, we relive the experience over and over, feeding it into our energy, unfiltered, which wreaks havoc and causes further distress.

Technique No. 17 Red Sofa Reclaiming Power and Self-Control

This technique allows you to regain full control, power, responsibility and authority within your whole self.

> ➢ Using the **Combined Technique No. 5**, from your core self, ground into Mother Earth, turn your master tap on to release emotions back to the Earth, and surrender thoughts to the higher mind.

> ➢ Set the intention that you are connecting with your pure soul essence and healing 'the lot'.

> ➢ In your stream of consciousness, imagine there is a lift.

> ➢ Step into the lift and press the button marked 'Higher Self'.

> ➢ When you reach the Higher Self level, step out of the lift into the Light of the Higher Self.

> ➢ Imagine in front of you a very large, red sofa. It's big enough to seat each and every aspect of you. (If you're 30 there will be 32 aspects of you: 30 + baby + foetal you.)

> ➢ Seat yourself on your sofa and invite all 32 (or whatever your number given your age) aspects to join you.

> ➢ Some may be shy, some may be withdrawn, some may not want to join you, and that's fine. Just get a sense of them.

> ➢ Taking your gaze down the sofa, look into the eyes of each and every aspect until you reach the foetal you. Then set the intention by saying out loud: *'Under the Laws of Cosmic Light, of All That Is and All That I AM, I reclaim full authority for all of us and for me. I reclaim full power for all of us and for me. I reclaim full responsibility for all of us and for me. I reclaim full control for all of us and for me. I reclaim all of this into the now. Any sense of duty and responsibility for others that I may have given you I reclaim now, and I release it in healing light to the Earth for transmutation. I return to others*

any power, authority, control, duty and responsibility I may have taken for or from them, or that they may have projected onto me. And with this energy, I open up to my stream of consciousness and I invite my soul essence into my existence.'

➤ Imagine each and every aspect of you held in pure soul essence.

➤ From this space, imagine each and every aspect of you connecting in with the purest form of Mother Earth, grounding through your soul essence into the heartbeat of Mother Earth.

➤ Get a sense of how each and every aspect of you realigns their vibration with the purest form of Earth.

➤ Become aware of the healing light of your soul bringing through cosmic light.

➤ Take as long as this healing needs and, when ready, take your awareness to the lift.

➤ Step into the lift and press the button marked 'Core Self'.

➤ Take your awareness back to your core self.

➤ Ground yourself into Mother Earth and give thanks.

Technique No. 18 Soul Group Healing Through Unconditional Love

The easiest way to clear these entanglements is healing through the soul group. *To do this, use the following technique.*

➤ Using the **Combined Technique No. 5**, from your core self, ground into Mother Earth, turn your master tap on to release emotions back to the Earth, and surrender thoughts to the higher mind.

➤ Set the intention that you are connecting with your pure soul essence and healing 'the lot'.

➤ In that stream of light, imagine there's a lift.

- Step into the lift and press the button for 'Soul Group'.
- Allow your energy and vibration to lift as you raise your vibration to the Soul Group level.
- When you reach the Soul Group level, step out of the lift and into the Light of the Soul Group.
- Imagine your light joining the Soul Group light.
- From this energy, set the intention that you're reaching up to the over soul and state: *'Under the Laws of Cosmic Light, of All That Is and All That I AM, I call upon the over soul and the whole soul group to hold my soul in light and the souls of others who wish to benefit from this healing at this moment in time. If it's in Divine highest order, and if it's for the greatest and highest good of all concerned, then I open this healing to the whole soul group so that our souls may know peace and may release back to the Earth all that needs to go to the Earth and to the light all that needs to go to the light. I ask my soul that any genetic, ancestral, karmic, soul group, past/present/future wounds, experiences and energies that are up for healing at this moment in time are forgiven, embraced in unconditional love and healed, in the light of the soul group and over soul, so that we may all know peace. So it is, it is done, so doth it be.'*
- Now imagine within you a deep sense of unconditional love being reawakened.
- Imagine your soul receiving grace, light and healing.
- Sense this light extending through all dimensions down into human form.
- Imagine this light extending down into the family vault and clearing and transmuting all energy, entanglements and enmeshments.
- Imagine this light bringing peace, balance and harmony to all meridians, chakras, glands and functions of the human body.

> ➤ Imagine your aura filling with pure soul essence and unconditional love.

> ➤ Take as long as this healing needs and, when ready, take your awareness to the lift.

> ➤ Step into the lift and press the button 'Core Self'.

> ➤ Take your awareness back to your core self.

> ➤ Ground yourself into Mother Earth and give thanks.

Quantum Entanglement

In his book *A New Earth*, Eckhart Tolle describes how awareness is the power that is concealed within the present moment. It is therefore very important that we reclaim our power and energy if we wish to stay in the present moment as self-empowered people.

Sometimes our connections are very deep. Quantum entanglement understands we are all connected as one. This is obvious when we've healed a past event only to find the person we've done the healing with phones or emails us. This demonstrates how deep the quantum entanglement really is. The following technique is a great way of bringing healing light into quantum entanglement.

Technique No. 19 Reclaiming Energy/Cord Cutting

This technique is based on the ancient Hawaiian Ho'oponopono practice of reconciliation and forgiveness, which recognises that on a soul level we are all one and, therefore, we bring healing to the whole soul group through healing ourselves.

> ➤ Using the **Combined Technique No. 5**, from your core self, ground into Mother Earth, turn your master tap on to release emotions back to the Earth, and surrender thoughts to the higher mind.

➢ Set the intention that you are connecting with your pure soul essence and healing 'the lot'.

➢ In that stream of light, imagine there's a lift.

➢ Step into the lift and press the button for 'Soul Group'. Allow your energy and vibration to lift as you raise your vibration to the Soul Group level.

➢ When you reach the Soul Group level, step out of the lift and into the Soul Group Light.

➢ Imagine your light joining the Soul Group Light.

➢ Imagine that opposite you is the soul of the person with whom you wish to heal.

➢ Ask your soul to acknowledge the soul of this person.

➢ From this energy, set the intention that you're reaching up to the over soul.

➢ Through this energy set the intention to open this healing to the whole soul group.

➢ Looking into the eyes of this other soul, state out loud, *'Under the Laws of Cosmic Light, of All That Is and All That I AM, I honour you and the light in you. I thank you for the lessons you've provided me with. Any contracts that our souls hold, I now ask that they are healed in cosmic light. Anything I projected onto you, or that you took from me through ego fear, I now reclaim and release to Mother Earth for transmutation. Anything you projected onto me I forgive and let go with ease, and anything I took from you I return to you transmuted in healing light. I fully reclaim and return all energies. I do this for the greatest and highest good of all concerned. So it is, it is done, so doth it be.'*

➢ And then state this, the Ho'oponopono mantra, three times: *'I am sorry, please forgive me, thank you, I love you.'*

➢ From this space, as described in **Technique No. 10**

Experiencing Hurts and Pains through the Soul, raise your higher heart with any wounds, scars or emotional hurts and surrender it to the whole soul group for healing and forgiveness.

➤ In this cosmic light, sense your heart raising its frequency to the soul group vibration of unconditional love and compassion.

➤ Allow this light to extend down into human form, dissolving and transmuting all attachments and enmeshments, be they in the form of hooks, cords or attachments (or whatever way they are presented to you).

➤ Imagine this energy like a double-edged sword of light. It is cutting through all connections in front of you, above you, behind you, to the right of you, to the left of you and underneath you.

➤ Set the intention that you are fully unattached to any negative energy on every level, every layer, every dimension and every realm, and through all existence in cosmic light.

➤ Sense the auric field repairing and healing any rips, tears or stagnant energies.

➤ Sense your whole core self being brought into full alignment with the conscious stream of light of forgiveness and unattachment to ego.

➤ Sense yourself held in the soul group consciousness of forgiveness.

➤ Take as long as this healing needs.

➤ Thank the other soul, the over soul and the whole soul group.

➤ Take your awareness to the lift.

➤ Stepping into the lift, press the button marked 'Core Self'.

➤ Take your awareness back to your core self.

➤ Ground yourself into Mother Earth and give thanks.

Whilst some of us are givers of energy and others are takers, the ideal situation would be to remain neutral. For those who are sensitive, or who are empaths and are naturally giving, the **Core Self Technique No. 1** is extremely beneficial, as it helps you to remain unattached and neutral to other people's emotions. It's also important to find a way to reclaim your energies. I have found that when leaving groups of people, an organisation, a building, an event or a situation, I can rebalance my energies through pure intention.

Technique No. 20 Intention to Unattach From Energy

➤ Using the **Combined Technique No. 5**, from your core self, ground into Mother Earth, turn your master tap on to release emotions back to the Earth, and surrender thoughts to the higher mind.

➤ Set the intention that you are connecting with your pure soul essence and healing 'the lot'.

➤ Become aware of the energy you wish to detach from. You may sense, know, feel or see the energy.

➤ Set the intention that you are detaching from this energy.

➤ Set the intention that whatever the mindset (conscious, subconscious or super-conscious) that attracted you to these energies, or attracted these energies to you, it is now being released up to your higher mind.

➤ State out loud: '*Under the Laws of Cosmic Light, of All That Is and All That I AM, I intend that I release to my higher mind the mindset of these energies. I separate from, detach and release all these energies, returning them either to the Earth for healing and transmutation or back to where they originated - if it's for the greatest and highest good of all concerned. I return and reclaim any energies intentionally or unintentionally taken or projected onto me so that my energy may remain neutral and held in pure conscious light and grounded into the Earth. So it is, it is done, so doth it be.*'

> ➢ Imagine yourself separating from the energy.
> ➢ Imagine yourself becoming detached from the energy.
> ➢ Imagine the energy falling away and releasing to the Earth.
> ➢ Imagine cosmic light transmuting all energies.
> ➢ Imagine yourself stepping deeper into the cosmic light.
> ➢ Take as long as this healing needs and, when ready, take your awareness back to your core self.
> ➢ Ground yourself into Mother Earth and give thanks.

We often use the phrase 'all-consuming' without fully realising just what it is we consume and absorb into our body, which we then find we're unable to digest. It is my understanding that a lot of the emotions sit in our gut unprocessed, either because we've taken on other people's energies, which become embroiled with our own leaving us unable to distinguish what is theirs and what is ours, or because we have a fear of letting go and therefore try to control events. As a result, we hold on even tighter to the emotions.

For those of you who are healers or therapists, there's a very simple exercise that will help you understand that the aura responds to, and carries the impression of, whatever is on the person's mind.

Exercise: Mental/Auric Connection

> ✳ Obtain crystals or stones in the shape of a sphere and a cube.
> ✳ Scan the person's aura and get a sense of how their aura feels.
> ✳ Ask them to hold the sphere in their hand and to connect with it.
> ✳ Ask them to imagine the sphere in their third eye.
> ✳ Whilst they are doing this, scan their aura to get a sense of the shape and form of the auric field.
> ✳ Remove the sphere from their hand and ask them to let it go from their mind.

* Place the cube in their hand and ask them to connect with it.
* Ask them to imagine the cube in their third eye.
* Whilst they are doing this, scan their aura to get a sense of the shape and form of the auric field.

This simple exercise will help you understand that whatever we're thinking about and connecting to becomes part of our auric field, and as soon as we disconnect from something it no longer has the same impact on our energy. This is true and very obvious in our relationships, where we take on people's worries and concerns. We feel duty-bound or have a sense of responsibility to do this, and feel that we are insensitive, cold and unloving unless we do it. This is what society and culture have nurtured in us over the years - a sense of guilt. These are the things we need to heal in this life to allow us the freedom to express our soul purpose in line with the Divine plan in this lifetime. This gives us the freedom to fully utilise our free will and purpose.

Chapter 5

HEART CHAKRA

The Heart Brings Balance Between What You Know Psychically and What You Sense Intuitively

The heart is the coming together of our creative expression, as well as our thinking and our physical embodiment of all that we do. We have the heart centre and the higher heart, which links us directly into our pure soul essence, our higher self, our Spirit. Some people may prefer to connect through the third eye, and that's fine, others may see the heart as the actualisation of the higher self, the expression of spiritual will expressed as unconditional love.

The heart is also where we hold fears, heartache, sorrow and grief, along with all the human emotions of the heart: jealousy, envy and rage. If our chakra system is balanced, whole and complete, then we can channel through our higher expression into our relationships with ourselves and others. If, however, our chakras are blocked then we manifest the physical attributes of the heart, such as jealousy, envy and unforgiveness. We've all witnessed events or situations where we've seen grown adults behaving like children throwing their toys out of the pram.

When Chaos Rules

When expression is blocked, it causes chaos in the mind and

restriction in the heart feeding down into the lower chakras. This chaos antagonises blockages, vulnerabilities and insecurities that may have been influenced or ingrained in us from childhood, prolonging events and restricting freedom and letting go. This chaos also ties us into habits, attitudes and beliefs that we've inherited, learned or even carried from past lives.

These restrictions and limitations stifle our expression, and we feed into wounds, pain and hurt from the past. We believe ourselves to be victims or martyrs who are controlled and manipulated by others. We see ourselves as caught up in a vicious cycle of negative feeling and thinking, feeling and thinking. It's as if we're a hamster on a wheel going round and round in the cycles of doom. Through this, we carry out our self-fulfilling prophecy of fear and failure, hurt and pain, victim and martyr. In so doing we block our expression of the spiritual will, and we block pleasure and joy. Instead, we feed into a sense of ego-based pride, stubbornness and unyielding beliefs and stifling traditions, otherwise known as unforgiveness. These are masked by the many names, blames and projections.

The Ancient Art of Forgiveness

As mentioned earlier, the Hawaiian healing process of Ho'oponopono ('I'm sorry, please forgive me, thank you, I love you') frees us up and eases the burden of pain, as does working with our inner child in the technique of reclaiming our power and working through the **Combination Technique No. 5.**

Sometimes, hurts and pains are too painful to remember and our ego finds every excuse and justification as to why we should hold these representations of just how much we've been damaged and of just how bad the other person is because of the terrible wrongs they've done us. Yet what really lurks behind is the expectation and the need to seek justice in the form of punishment. Old beliefs, maybe from past lives, maybe from this life, and the belief in Hell and damnation and that God will punish sits in our heart centre creating in us a sense of judge and jury, meting out punishments and fuelling the victim and persecutor mentality.

Family feuds

We've all experienced or witnessed family feuds carried from generation to generation. We hear of countries at war, where hatred is carried on many years after the battle. This fills our hearts with contempt and blocks any hope of compassion, tolerance and acceptance of our differences. Yet in order to live in today's multicultural world, we need to develop a greater tolerance and acceptance of these differences. Sometimes, the differences that we see in others are a reminder of a person, place or thing that may have hurt us in the past. As a result, we project all our feelings and emotions onto a representation. This is where we project all our fear, hurt and pain. And sometimes, it is the unlikeliest of suspects, those nearest and dearest to us, who feel our wrath. Remember, this gets locked into your cells, forming the family inheritance that is passed from generation to generation. This is what will influence the mindset of your children and their children in their decision making and choices in life. Ask yourself the question: *Is this what I want for future generations to come?*

So, having a base chakra where you feel strong and confident, safe and secure, a sacral chakra free of guilt and a solar plexus free of shame helps in opening the heart centre so that we may release any blame and any unforgiveness. This lets our soul essence bring joy, pleasure, tolerance, acceptance and unconditional love into the auric field.

As you may have experienced when using the sphere and cube shapes in the mental/auric field scanning exercise, the instant reaction of the aura to the mindset is amazing. Scan the person's aura when they are worried about an event. Use the techniques mentioned above to help them let go, release the mindset and focus on forgiveness and acceptance of differences. Then scan the person's aura when they are in a total state of bliss. It's a beautiful exercise to scan someone's aura and sense the freedom and flow of energy when they're in this state.

Technique No. 21 Channelling Rainbow Light and Opening to Unconditional Love

As mentioned earlier, intention is very powerful. Whatever we are thinking of or wherever we focus our attention on, this energy will be reflected in our auric field.

- ➤ Using the **Combined Technique No. 5**, from your core self, ground into Mother Earth, turn your master tap on to release emotions back to the Earth, and surrender thoughts to the higher mind.

- ➤ Set the intention that you are connecting with your pure soul essence and healing 'the lot'.

- ➤ State out loud: *'Under the Laws of Cosmic Light, of All That Is and All That I AM, I intend to be a clear channel of heartfelt soul expression of compassion and unconditional love. So it is, it is done, so doth it be.'*

- ➤ Through your stream of consciousness, imagine a beautiful rainbow of light descend upon you.

- ➤ Imagine this rainbow surrounding your energy and wrapping you in every colour of the rainbow.

- ➤ Feel red, orange, yellow, green, blue, indigo and violet colours being absorbed into your aura.

- ➤ Take your awareness to your heart centre and breathe in this pure light.

- ➤ With each breath, draw a colour of rainbow light into your heart centre.

- ➤ Breathe red into your heart centre and allow it to settle in the base chakra.

➢ Breathe orange into your heart centre and allow it to settle in the sacral chakra.

➢ Breathe yellow into your heart centre and allow it to settle in the solar plexus.

➢ Breathe green into your heart centre and allow it to settle in the heart centre.

➢ Breathe blue into your heart centre and allow it to settle in the throat chakra.

➢ Breathe indigo into your heart centre and allow it to settle in the third eye.

➢ Breathe violet into your heart centre and allow it to settle in the crown chakra.

➢ Imagine the light and energy of each colour travelling through your heart into the many, many layers and depths of its existence.

➢ Then, travelling from your heart centre to the relevant chakra, imagine this rainbow taking you right to the core of unconditional love within your heart centre.

➢ Imagine this unconditional love within your heart centre being reawakened in light.

➢ Imagine this unconditional love travelling from your heart centre to all the chakras.

➢ Imagine this unconditional love filling your auric field.

➢ Imagine you are at the core of this unconditional love.

➢ Imagine, as you seat yourself in this core, that you merge with this aspect of your being.

➢ Sense yourself empowered and removed beyond the emotions of the heart into the stillness and calmness of this core.

➢ Sense the contentment that comes with this unconditional love.

➢ In this space, take your awareness to your feet and the roots that connect you with Mother Earth.

➢ Allow this rainbow light of unconditional love to pour from your feet down into the heartbeat of Mother Earth.

➢ Connect in with the nurturing love, safety, security, power and vitality that Mother Earth has to offer you.

➢ Sense this as a pulse, up through your roots to your feet.

➢ Sense this energy up through your feet to your shins and calves.

➢ Sense this energy in your knees, thighs and buttocks.

➢ Sense it connecting into your base chakra, activating in you a newfound sense of nurturing, safety and security, which is formed through unconditional love.

➢ Sense this love like that between a mother and child because that's what you are, a child of the Earth.

➢ Sense this nurturing, unconditional love extending up into the sacral chakra, reawakening in you the belief and the trust that all your needs are met freely and unconditionally.

➢ In this profound, empowered state, sense the energy surging into your solar plexus and reawakening in you (or unlocking in you) the pure power of Mother Earth that you connect into in your formation as a human being.

➢ Sense this power merging with your willpower and transmuting ego-based power into core-self empowerment.

➢ Imagine this power of the Earth anchoring, strengthening and reinforcing your core strength.

➢ From this heartfelt place of pureness and oneness, sense this unconditional love gently lasering through every emotional layer of your heart.

➢ Imagine all heartfelt emotions being cleared and healed of all hurts, pains, wounds and scars.

➢ Imagine all blocks of unforgiveness and all emotions of the heart coming right through into your place of unconditional love.

➢ This is opening in you an expansion and expression through which your soul essence can sing.

➢ Imagine that this is the expression that you carry from the heart up to the throat chakra, activating pure soul expression.

➢ Sense this expression influencing your third eye, activating within wisdom and a profound sense of knowing.

➢ Sense this extending up into your crown chakra, up into your truth, into your higher mind.

➢ Imagine it unlocking the will of your soul and feel that willpower extending down through all the chakras and merging with the power within, your free will.

➢ Imagine this as a channel of pure expression in which to safely (with purity and clarity) and fully exert your authority and free will creatively in line with your soul purpose and the Divine plan.

➢ Imagine this channel of pure expression impacting on your manifestations through Mother Earth.

➢ Take as long as this healing needs and, when ready, take your awareness back to your core self.

➢ Ground yourself into Mother Earth and give thanks.

Sometimes, we take an instant dislike to someone. I know of a person who has a very strong hatred for their brother-in-law and cannot be in their company without intense emotions surfacing. This creates tension that results in arguments, which isn't very nice for those near and dear to witness. This hatred extends back to a religious past life where this person was a monk who died at the hands of another monk during a massacre. The killer, in this life, is the brother-in-law.

Our souls carry into this life patterns of unforgiveness and karmic debt. They don't all have to be as profound as the one mentioned above, but it does show how our subconscious mind influences our feelings and emotions. Whether you believe in past lives or not, you can see how generation after generation have carried hatred, bitterness and venom in their hearts for events and incidents that they've had no conscious part in. And yet they hold the hurt and pain through stubborn pride. There have been many wars and battles resulting in grief and loss, and yet forgiveness is the key.

Technique No. 22 Healing Family Wounds

➢ Using the **Combined Technique No. 5**, from your core self, ground into Mother Earth, turn your master tap on to release emotions back to the Earth, and surrender thoughts to the higher mind.

➢ Set the intention that you are connecting with your pure soul essence and healing 'the lot'.

➢ Reconnect with the place of unconditional love within your heart centre (which you connected to in Technique No. 18).

➢ From this place, state out loud: *'Under the Laws of Cosmic light, of All That Is and All That I AM, I intend to free myself from this wound. So it is, it is done, so doth it be.'*

➢ Imagine a beautiful golden master key in your place of unconditional love that allows you to access the deep recesses of the family vault.

➢ Imagine from your heart centre that you find your access point to the family vault. Be aware that you are coming from your purest state of unconditional love and unattachment.

➢ Imagine opening the vault and take your awareness to this wound.

➢ Imagine the wound held in light.

➢ Set the intention that this wound is offered up for healing to the whole soul group.

➢ Set the intention that you are reclaiming your power and energy by stating out loud: *'Under the Laws of Cosmic Light, of All That Is and All That I AM, I reclaim my power, I reclaim my energy. Anything I contributed towards this wound I reclaim and release to the Earth for transmutation. Anything I created and co-created through this energy I reclaim, surrendering to Spirit what needs to go to Spirit, and to the Earth what needs to go to the Earth. I surrender the mindset of this wound to my higher mind. I am free and I release you into the light. So it is, it is done, so doth it be.'*

➢ Complete the Hawaiian healing process of Ho'oponopono: *'I'm sorry, please forgive me, thank you, I love you.'* Repeat this three times.

➢ Imagine this wound dissolving and in its place is pure soul essence and Divine Light.

➢ Sense your heart centre expanding and reclaiming the light and unconditional love.

➢ Take as long as this healing needs and, when ready, take your awareness back to your core self.

➢ Ground yourself into Mother Earth and give thanks.

What I love about energy healing is the instant reaction to pure intention. Students and clients are often concerned that they need to reconnect, or reform old relationships - which they don't want to do - in order to make amends and put things right. Because we are all one on the quantum level, energy healing works without having to make contact in person. Through setting an intention to forgive, to heal and to let go, the higher levels of our being cascades down into the physical form instantly.

When teaching, I encourage students to scan the aura of a person while that person brings up a relationship issue and heals it using the numerous techniques within this book. The feedback from the person scanning is that they can sense huge shifts of energy and change. These are almost instantaneous in the auric field and are followed by a very smooth flow of energy.

Working through the deep levels of your being and opening your heart in total forgiveness brings in so much love and light. Using conscious intent heals our patterns and history. Some people report the synchronicities that happen after a healing, where their perception shifts and they find themselves encountering new experiences they never thought possible. They open up to new ways of thinking and find themselves forming new relationships and experiencing transformational shifts beyond their wildest dreams.

We all have friends or family members who have difficulty in finding a partner, and when they do each one displays the same patterns and traits of the one before, bringing up old wounds and hurts. However, once they start to heal those wounds and hurts instead of suppressing them, opening up to healing and forgiveness of themselves and others, they find that they are attracting different people into their lives and forming very different relationships.

There is the old belief that the universe will keep providing us with the lessons we need to learn until such a time as we learn them, and this I do believe. Using these techniques helps bypass the ego, allowing you to find for yourself the lessons you need to learn, and bringing the healing in without you having to endure the previous patterns of prolonged endurance and fighting against the inevitable. It truly is a case of mind over matter. If you don't mind, then it doesn't matter.

We Take Our Environment in Through Our Senses

As mentioned earlier, Dr Jill Bolte Taylor in her book, *My Stroke of Insight,* says we are multi-sensory beings and take our environment in through our senses before giving it thought. If our senses are saturated, then this can result in ultra-sensitive sensory overload, and our feelings can take us on cycles and patterns of old wounds and hurts.

I've witnessed clients and students who, in healing a current relationship issue while at the same time healing a childhood pain, created a domino effect resulting in a very safe release of an avalanche of emotions, the end result being that the current issue no longer had dominance over how they felt and thought. Who we are today is very much underpinned by our past. And whilst we can't change the past, we can change how we feel about it through forgiveness and healing of the emotions. This impacts our thoughts and thinking, helping us to have a different perspective on things.

Forgiving the past (which influences your now) allows you to hold that space of inner core strength, personal power, open-centeredness and bliss. And as we all know, our future is built on the now, and if we want to avoid reliving the past, then the calmer and clearer our now is, the better. Our expression of our now is what influences our creativity.

Chapter 6

THYMUS CHAKRA

The Activator of Consciousness

The thymus chakra or the higher heart links in with soul purpose and how we bring this into our lives as our service to humanity. It is the synthesis of the lower chakras and the expression of all that's gone before, so the more we heal the lower chakras, the clearer the expression of soul purpose and light. In certain esoteric traditions, it is also understood that this is where we hold ancestral addictions.

The clearing of the thymus chakra is very important in helping us to find equilibrium in the now as, without our realisation, we are a by-product of everything that's gone before us. As mentioned in previous chapters, epigenetic studies indicate that we carry the emotional baggage of our forefathers.

Impact of Planetary Shifts

It is also my understanding - via my limited knowledge of astrology - that each and every planetary shift impacts greatly on Mother Earth's energies. As we are of the Earth and connected in through our ancestral lineage and karmic past life links (which hold the energetic imprint of all our experiences and all that's gone before us), any impact or planetary pressure on these Earth imprints brings these karmic debts or the ancestral baggage up into our energy field. We have the free will to view this as part of our life lessons, and we can either heal and transmute these energies or continue the karmic and ancestral cycles and patterns of fear, anger, etc., and become more enmeshed in negative energies and traits.

These amazing times we live in provide the right planetary alignments to allow us to disembroil, unattach and let go with grace and ease, therefore freeing us to be our own true self – and it's the thymus chakra that houses the self. It's our access to our light, our higher living. I have found the following technique to be extremely beneficial.

Technique No. 23 Healing Ancestral Energy Links Through the Family Tree

If you have access to your family tree then use it for this technique. If not, draw out a rough chart using the names of ancestors. If you don't know them, use their title, i.e., mother, father, grandmother and grandfather, etc. Always work from your core self and purest light.

➤ Using the **Combined Technique No. 5**, from your core self, ground into Mother Earth, turn your master tap on to release emotions back to the Earth, and surrender thoughts to the higher mind.

➤ Set the intention that you are connecting with your pure soul essence and healing 'the lot'.

➤ Take your awareness to your heart centre of unconditional love and work from this place (which you connected to in **Technique No. 18**).

➤ Write your name on the top of the page and write your mother's and father's names on the line below it. Use whatever terms you use for your parents and grandparents. Personalise it for you. I suggest you work back at least six generations. You may even wish to add more.

➢ Set the intention that when you draw out, or look through your ancestral chart, you are becoming aware of energy connection points with any ancestral links that are prominent in your life at this moment in time. Through this intention, we're creating an energy chain link down the ancestral line.

➢ Become aware that each ancestor represents a point in your existence, and these points of energy feed into your energy flow through your subconscious mind. This is how we take on their emotional baggage (epigenetics).

➢ Imagine that you can control the direction and destiny of negative emotions and energies by placing a tap on each energy point.

➢ Set the intention that instead of flowing into you, this energy goes straight to Mother Earth for transmutation.

➢ Connect in with your heart centre of unconditional love and bring in the rainbow of light.

➢ Imagine this rainbow flowing through your ancestral lines into the energy connection points, bringing in pure, healing love and light.

➢ If necessary, complete the Hawaiian healing technique: 'I am sorry, please forgive me, thank you, I love you.' Repeat it three times.

➢ Take as long as this healing needs and, when ready, take your awareness back to your core self.

➢ Ground yourself into Mother Earth and give thanks.

Note: *All the time that you are using this technique you are clearing through your taps and surrendering to your higher mind.*

Every time I do this exercise, I see it as an unravelling of ancestral emotions, which exit my physical form through the front and back of the thymus chakra, allowing me in my pure self to emerge anew. Clearing this chakra helps you to realign with your true self and frees you up to deal with the stuff your soul wants you to deal with in this lifetime. It also helps you to focus on your soul purpose in line with the Divine plan.

Clearing the thymus chakra helps clear the way for you to step into your pure stream of consciousness, free of the limitations, beliefs and patterns of your ancestors and also free from those of past lives. You are literally freeing yourself from influences that have hindered and blocked your energy flow up to now. This healing allows you to access your true light and to bring more of this light down into your heart centre.

In addition, feeding through compassion helps bring tolerance and acceptance into the other chakras, freeing you to live your life and your relationships through your soul light and not your shadow. This is pure soul expression emerging through the core self, helping you to identify beyond ego who you truly are. It is only when we allow ourselves to access this point of self that we can really accept and appreciate the benefit of unattachment. The following imagery has helped me to fully submerge myself in this light.

Kebab Analogy

Consider life where you are in your purest form of soul essence as like a beautiful silver skewer, and consider every experience from the moment you enter the birth canal - right throughout life and including fear, shame, guilt, blame, heartache, grief, vulnerability, insecurity, worry and anxiety - as pieces of dross, forming meat-like contributions that we hold onto and try to process because we are reluctant to give them up. Imagine these building up on the skewer into what resembles our very own kebab. And anytime somebody threatens to slice through this dross, we take it very personally and either become the victim or the defender, adding even more dross to an already fattened kebab.

Using this imagery and having the knowledge that every hurt, pain and negative experience we hold onto is just that, dross, helps us to step more and more into the light of that silver skewer, which represents us stepping more and more into our core self. This very intention allows us to become unattached and to see experiences and events for what they are, making letting go easier. Imagine the kebab falling away from the skewer and disintegrating, allowing the true self to emerge and fully shine. Using the kebab analogy as you observe the ancestral energy points, clearing through the thymus chakra, fully supports the letting go because it was never yours in the first place - you just inherited it. Healing the thymus chakra also allows us the ability to separate and tolerate.

Technique No. 24 Thymus Chakra Healing Using Fluorite Crystals

For those of you who may be interested in incorporating crystals into your healing, rainbow fluorite is a lovely crystal for working with the thymus chakra. This is a basic **Seal of Solomon technique**, which I learnt whilst studying crystal therapies. For this technique, you will need seven fluorite crystals.

> Using the Combined Technique No. 5, from your core self, ground into Mother Earth, turn your master tap on to release emotions back to the Earth, and surrender thoughts to the higher mind.

> Set the intention that you are connecting with your pure soul essence and healing 'the lot'.

> Lie on the floor and surround yourself with six of the crystals in the following format:

  o One above the crown chakra, one to the right of your right knee and one to the left of your left knee; this forms a triangle.

  o Now place a crystal beneath your feet, one to the left of your left shoulder and one to the right of your right shoulder; this forms a second overlapping triangle.

o   These combined create the Seal of Solomon.

➢ Lie in this crystal grid and place the seventh crystal on your thymus chakra, midway between your heart and throat (you may need to use a piece of cello tape to hold it in place).

➢ Surrender to your true core self and allow yourself to fully submit to this light and absorb it into your entire being.

➢ Fully embrace your soul essence so that you may be your true self.

➢ Take as long as this healing needs and, when ready, step out of the crystal grid.

➢ Take your awareness back to your core self.

➢ Ground yourself into Mother Earth and give thanks.

Chapter 7

THROAT CHAKRA

Spoken and Unspoken Vibrations of Mind and Matter

The throat chakra is located on the part of the body that connects mind and matter. It's where we express our human form and also where we can express the channel of our Divine Light. This is an outlet for our shadow aspects. This is how we verbally relate in all our relationships. Through this, we create oaths, allegiances, agreements, promises, vows and verbal contracts. Through the vibration of sound we create form and we co-create with others, either becoming embroiled and enmeshed through our negative expression, or expressing our love or forgiveness, thus freeing and releasing through our positive light.

A base chakra of fear, a sacral chakra of guilt, a solar plexus of shame, a heart filled with grief and a thymus blocking our true self results in expressions of form that are negative and fear-based. They lock us into negative beliefs and patterns that have influenced these energies in the first place - hence the continuous cycles that we are so familiar with and yet resent so much. On the other hand, a base chakra of strength and safety, a sacral of desire, a solar plexus of power and a heart of joy means the light of the true self expresses itself fully and reflects the reality we desire.

Free Will

It is my understanding that we all have free will. We get to choose who, what, when, where, why and how we go through life. It is also my understanding that we have destiny. This may be in the form of the many lessons and experiences that life offers us. Some may look at these as life's knocks, others may see them as life's opportunity for growth.

The journey of the soul is the expression of our life here on Earth. In order to find harmony between free will and destiny, we as humans need to accept and embrace our *human* aspects and *being* aspects, which combine together to form us as a *human being*. If we allow the experiences life offers us to be seen as a union of *higher self* advising *ego self* and combining destiny and free will together, then the choices we make through the use of willpower will be our expression. This is the growth our soul needs to flourish.

Energy, Frequency and Vibration

Croatian inventor, Nikola Tesla (1856 – 1943), once said: *"If you want to find the secrets of the universe, think in terms of energy, frequency and vibration."* Most of Tesla's ideas and designs were patented by other inventors. He is also credited as being a pioneer in the discovery and development of X-ray technology, radar technology and the rotating magnetic field. Science through quantum physics now understands that everything is energy and that numerous laws bind us. The law of vibration states that everything in the universe is in constant movement, nothing rests. Because we vibrate on different frequencies we feel separate, yet we are all one field of energy. Lynn McTaggart talks about this in her book *The Field*.

These frequencies either resonate or repel the energies around us. When we put expression with intention, this is what gives it force. It's a bit like putting the key in the ignition of a very powerful car and the power only kicking in when we switch on the motor.

Every utterance creates energy and the thoughts behind it, i.e., the intention gives it the force, so be very careful of your words because they leave an energy imprint.

Energy Footprints

In schools today, we teach children all about carbon footprints, and the importance of cleaning up the Earth from a physical and material perspective. This is very important, as we've seen the devastating effect that global warming has had on our rivers, oceans and wildlife, and yet our thoughts can be toxic too.

We have all fallen foul of the toxic comments, the snide remarks and the hurtful blows of words from our loved ones, be they in the form of rejection, hatred or anger. These render us vulnerable and insecure, and in this unsafe feeling, we become defensive. Our retorts can be equally negative, creating and co-creating vibrations and frequencies that we project onto each other. And, depending on the force we use to deal these blows, they can be very damaging on the auric field.

Equally, a soothing word, a compliment, a sentence of praise can make us feel empowered, loved and nurtured. It is my understanding that thoughts themselves create energy, but this becomes amplified and given a form of its own when sent out into the universe. That's why affirmations can be very powerful things.

Affirmations

Sometimes people struggle with affirmations and intentions, This is because the subconscious mind overrules the conscious intent. So whilst we verbally commit throughout our life, through vows and oaths, etc., in some circumstances we put our heart and soul into an experience and are so committed to it that it still holds firm even in death, causing us to carry it into our present life, where it influences us subconsciously. It's important that we clear these contracts and utterances by verbalising to the universe our intent to bring them forward and to nullify them through transmuting light. This frees us up energetically to create through positive affirmations and manifest through pure intent and light. I have found the following technique very useful.

Technique No. 25 Nullifying Soul Contracts

> ➢ Using the **Combined Technique No. 5**, from your core self, ground into Mother Earth, turn your master tap on to release emotions back to the Earth, and surrender thoughts to the higher mind.

> ➢ Set the intention that you are connecting with your pure soul essence and that you are healing 'the lot'.

> ➢ In that stream of light, imagine there's a lift.

> ➢ Step into the lift and press the button for 'Soul Group'.

> ➢ Allow your energy and vibration to lift as you raise your vibration to the Soul Group level.

> ➢ When you reach the Soul Group level step out of the lift and into the Light of the Soul Group.

> ➢ Imagine your light joining the soul group light.

> ➢ From this energy, set the intention that you're reaching up to the over soul and state: *'Under the Laws of Cosmic Light, of All That Is and All That I AM, I ask my soul and the whole soul group to hold my soul in pure light. I intend here and now to seek forgiveness and to offer forgiveness so that cosmic healing light may be directed to all utterances, thoughts and intentions and to all vows, oaths, allegiances, agreements and promises made in this life, past or future. This includes all binds, ties, shackles or restrictions, along with any magic, curses and spells. I wish to release all the experiences and memories our souls may hold, conscious or subconscious, in relation to these so that my soul and the soul group may know peace. I ask that any soul contracts that are now up for*

release are nullified and released into the light, and I ask that any soul contracts that are current are held in Divine cosmic light so that they are fulfilled through soul expression of unconditional love and light. I seek forgiveness and I offer forgiveness. I do this for the greatest and highest good of all concerned. So it is, it is done, so forever doth it be.'

➤ Imagine the contracts being nullified and dissolved in Divine cosmic light.

➤ Imagine any current contracts held in Divine cosmic light.

➤ Take as long as this healing needs and, when ready, step back into the lift and press the button marked 'core self'.

➤ Take your awareness back to your core self.

➤ Ground yourself into Mother Earth and give thanks.

It is likely that as souls over the last six thousand years, our incarnations may have had a religious or spiritual flavour and our death in that lifetime may harbour some prejudices, bigotry and/or patterns of thinking that influence our behaviours in this lifetime. So, if a life of authority and responsibility for the consciousness of others through religious vows can sometimes influence the archetype of martyrdom in this life, I like to think that we can cancel form through form.

For some this may be where they are *locked* into vows or promises made in a past life. Such as vow of poverty, vow of chastity, or a promise to remain faithful and wait for a particular loved one. Influencing decisions or choices in this lifetime.

I also like to think that bringing past deeds to the surface whilst holding a higher frequency in relation to it, such as forgiveness or compassion, will override and transmute previous intent, otherwise known as healing. The word 'sorry' has such a powerful healing frequency, which is recognised worldwide. It penetrates deeply. It heals wounds. Sometimes the ego and our deep sense of pride can prevent us from apologising face to face, and yet it's the intent and the verbalisation that can travel any distance, realm or dimension, for its power can be felt through the whole cosmos.

So, working soul to soul, from your stream of consciousness and stating the Hawaiian Ho'oponopono healing mantra to anybody, anytime and anywhere carries the healing. You just need to open up, clear the thoughts and allow the feelings to flow. Through grounding in with Mother Earth and using the master tap technique, you set the intention that all your chakras work in alignment with pure Mother Earth, enabling you to forgive and let go.

The throat chakra in its vibration communicates through the mind, heart and core. So if your mind is filled with negative thoughts, your heart is blocked, and your core is the ego force of will. That's what you create in your reality versus the mindset of the higher mind, the heart centre of the true self and the desire to do Divine will.

Chapter 8

THIRD EYE CHAKRA

Inner Vision

The third eye chakra, also known as the brow chakra, is also referred to as the seat of intuition, as the centre for inner wisdom and vision. It enables us to look within and see ourselves beyond our self-identity and our limited mind and ego patterns. Inner vision may present itself as intuition, symbolic thinking, insights, impressions, imagination, dreams and visions. All of which impact greatly on our thinking and feeling and depending on the level of awareness we work from this may be either negative or positive. Sometimes, we have difficulty in understanding our thinking and may even feel very blinkered in our beliefs, unaware that our ancestral experiences and past lives may be influencing our beliefs, habits and attitudes in this lifetime.

This simple exercise helps you to understand that whatever you are thinking about impacts on your energy. This is also known as *mind over matter*. So if you *don't mind* it *won't matter!* Just change your thinking.

Feeling Your Thinking Exercise

* Become aware of your brain inside your head.

* Sense its outline, shape and form.

* Take your awareness to your thoughts and thinking.

* Get a sense of the energy of your mind, which is your brain in action.

* Get a sense of the flow of this energy, and any rigidity of its direction or projection.

* Get a sense of how your energy feels as a result of your mind.

* Now take your thoughts to a very positive or funny incident or event, and get a sense of the direction or projection of your thoughts.

* Get a sense of how your energy feels, in particular how your body feels with these thoughts.

* Pause for a moment.

* Take your thoughts to a negative or fear-based incident or event. Get a sense of the direction or projection.

* Get a sense of how your energy feels, in particular how your body feels with these thoughts.

*Now that you've brought up negative emotions use the **Combined Technique** to clear these (**Technique No. 5**).*

The mind is very powerful and can instantly fuel us with love or hate, negative or positive, and yet the soul is more powerful - if only we were to embrace it and listen to the inner guidance it offers us. Working with the soul group and the over soul helps us heal so that the soul may freely relinquish soul wounds and karmic debt to the Earth for transmutation.

Whilst the mind is powerful, the higher mind is our true power and potential. This is because the higher mind brings wisdom and light and goes beyond illusion and false perception.

Technique No. 26 Freeing the Mind

This technique is based on **Technique No. 4**, Surrendering to the Higher Mind. Although we will look at freeing the mind from the mindset around money and finances, etc, you can adapt it to work on any mindset you wish to heal. *Form your own questions, using key trigger words relevant to your situation.*

This technique starts off differently from the others in that we work on identifying beliefs, thoughts, patterns of thinking and our feelings in relation to these, etc., before we turn on the taps or surrender to the higher mind.

> ➢ Using the **Core Self Technique No. 1**, from your core self, ground into Mother Earth.

> ➢ Take your awareness to your brain in your head, get a sense of its shape and how it feels.

> ➢ Take your awareness to your thoughts about money. Do you worry about bills and/or the cost of living? Do you struggle financially? Are you in debt?

> ➢ Do you consider that your lifestyle is seriously limited by lack of money? Are you stuck with no way out due to financial commitments and lack of funds?

> ➢ Get a sense of what emotions and feelings this brings up in you. Are you anxious or nervous? Do you feel fear, dread or anger?

> ➢ Does this bring up any memories of past experiences around money? Perhaps defaulting on payments, borrowing from friends or family, a failed business, bankruptcy, etc.?

> ➢ Get a sense of how and where your physical body responds to these thoughts.

> ➢ Take your awareness to your beliefs about money. Money is there to be spent/I'm hopeless with money/The rich get richer, and the poor get poorer/My family never had money/It's selfish to want money/I don't deserve wealth/Mum and dad will help.

➤ Take your awareness to your family beliefs around money. You have to work hard for money/Money is the root of all evil/Spend it whilst you have it/You can't take it with you when you die.

➤ Get a sense of how and where your physical body responds to these thoughts.

➤ Answer the following: *'Do you believe this belief?'* If so, how much of this belief is yours? If none of it is, how much of other people's beliefs around money do you allow to influence your mindset?

➤ Get a sense of how much of this feeds into your reality.

➤ Set the intention that you are connecting with your pure soul essence and that you are healing 'the lot'.

➤ Turn on your master tap and release all emotions back to Mother Earth for transmutation.

➤ Take your awareness to your conscious and subconscious mind.

➤ State out loud to the cosmos: *'Under the Laws of Cosmic Light, of All That Is and All That I AM, I intend here and now to fully surrender to my higher mind my relationship with money, my beliefs, influences, mindset and all conscious and subconscious thoughts. I surrender any vows of poverty or thoughts of lack. I intend to heal 'the lot' and fully embrace the mindset of abundance and flow. I do this for the greatest and highest good of all concerned. So it is, it is done, so doth it be.'*

➤ Now take your awareness to your higher mind located above and unattached to any lower mindsets.

➤ You may wish to imagine your higher mind like a beautiful silver crown encrusted with jewels of your choice.

➤ Set the intention that you direct your conscious and subconscious thoughts up into this crown, surrendering everything to your higher mind and letting go with trust.

Follow through with **Technique No. 27 Embracing Your Higher Mind into Your Mind Heart and Core** *to download the mindset of abundance. Adapt the wording to include abundance.*

Control Blocks Trust

Some people have difficulty letting go of control, but let me explain that this technique is similar to having your own personal assistant who is wise, just, and works for your highest and greatest good. They know everything you need and how to go about it. I liken this technique to delegating everything to my higher mind, knowing that everything will be sorted in accordance with my soul purpose and the Divine plan. All I have to do is trust.

For those of you who may have issues around trust, then I suggest you use this technique to work on issues of *distrust*, examining memories where you made bad choices, feared consequences, feared the unknown and/or feared losing control. Work on this technique, surrendering all conscious, subconscious and super conscious thoughts and ancestral thoughts up to your higher self.

If the lower chakras are blocked or depleted, then our thoughts and thinking reflect this, whether or not these are conscious or subconscious thoughts. The more we clear the more intuitive we become, the more intuitive we become the more we develop our sensitivities and sixth sense. The more developed our sixth sense is, the more we tune into other dimensions and frequencies - we raise our frequencies to those of the 4th, 5th and higher dimensions.

Searching for a Meaning to Life

More and more people are searching for a higher meaning to life. Developing regular spiritual practices helps us to achieve this, and it also assists our soul's growth and expansion. This enables us to vibrate at a much higher frequency, as our soul expands through the expression of light. Yet for some, fears and vulnerabilities are seen as the dark night of the soul, rendering us powerless and inculcating a futile approach in the soul's quest for peace. This locks us into the hells that we create for ourselves here on Earth. But what we fail to realise is that this is just another form of mindset.

We are constantly creating, co-creating and manifesting. Thanks to the research carried out by doctors such as Jill Bolte Taylor and Joe Dispenza, we now understand that changing our thinking changes our reality. Every thought is followed by a chemical. These chemicals influence our hormone development, which impacts on our whole biological process - all stemming from thought. Every cell in our body stores emotions. As mentioned previously, Dr Candace Pert's book *Molecules of Emotion* and Dr David Hamilton's book *Is Your Life Mapped Out?* both look at how we carry the energy of our forefathers, influencing how we feel, think and who we are. And yet, our higher mind knows our true self.

Our higher mind overrides, overpowers and transmutes the lower mind, awakening in our cells our perfection as Divine sparks of light. This is available to us in the form of downloads and, as with anything in life, it is our destiny, although we also have free will. We can use this free will to block it through fear and limiting beliefs, or we can use it to be open to it and fully embrace it, allowing it to empower us in our light.

Technique No. 27 Embracing Higher Mind into Your Mind, Heart and Core

This technique can be adapted to download any mindset you desire, simply alter the wording to suit your requirements. For example, I intend that I have the mindset of abundance/I intend that I have the mindset of joy/I intend that I have the mindset of wisdom etc., and reflect these changes in the wording throughout the technique. This technique brings your intention, focus and will into perfect alignment with the mindset you desire.

- Using the **Combined Technique No. 5**, from your core self, ground into Mother Earth, turn your master tap on to release emotions back to the Earth, and surrender thoughts to the higher mind.

- Set the intention that you are connecting with your pure soul essence and healing 'the lot'.

- Take your awareness to your stream of consciousness and imagine the higher mind as that beautiful silver crown.

- Set the intention that your intention, focus and will are in perfect alignment with your higher mind.

- Imagine your higher mind working with you as you reach up to your higher mind and download the mindset of *unconditional love, compassion, tolerance and acceptance for self and others* into your lower mind.

- Allow your lower mind to receive these higher mind patterns and let them settle into a natural state of comfort and fit.

- State out loud the following intention: *'Under the Laws of Cosmic Light, of All That Is and All That I AM, I fully embrace my higher mind patterns of unconditional love, compassion, tolerance and acceptance for myself and others into my lower mind. Surrendering fully any thoughts and thinking that may contradict these new lighter vibrational patterns up into my higher mind, so that I may be open to receiving higher guidance and that I may know peace, wisdom and light. I do this for my greatest and highest good and the greatest and highest good of all concerned. So it is, it is done, so doth it be.'*

- Get a sense of your mind filling with the patterns of unconditional love, compassion, tolerance and acceptance for self and others. Fully embrace these patterns into your lower mind, knowing that all intentions, focus and will are in perfect alignment with this higher vibrational mindset.

➢ Allow these patterns of unconditional love, compassion, tolerance and acceptance for self and others to extend down into your heart centre.

➢ Sense your heart centre opening and embracing these lighter vibrational patterns, knowing that all intentions, focus and will are in perfect alignment with this higher vibrational mindset.

➢ Allow these patterns of unconditional love, compassion, tolerance and acceptance to extend down into your gut, and fully embrace them into your core.

➢ From this place, imagine your willpower stepping into these patterns of unconditional love, compassion, tolerance and acceptance, knowing that all intentions, focus and will are in perfect alignment with these higher vibrations.

➢ State out loud the following intention: *'Under the Laws of Cosmic Light, of All That Is and All That I AM, I intend that I fully embrace these higher vibrational patterns of unconditional love, compassion, tolerance and acceptance for myself and others into my mind, heart and core. I intend that all intentions, focus and will are in perfect alignment with my soul purpose and the Divine plan. I do this for the greatest and highest good of all concerned. So it is, it is done, so forever doth it be.'*

➢ Take as long as this healing needs and, when ready, take your awareness back to your core self, knowing that all intentions, focus and will are in perfect alignment with your soul purpose and the Divine plan.

➢ Ground yourself into Mother Earth and give thanks.

Chapter 9

CROWN CHAKRA

Gateway to Higher Consciousness

Our crown chakra connects us to universal truth, higher concepts, higher ideals and higher mind. Being open to the higher mind and higher thinking helps bring pure soul essence and a profound peace of mind into all forms of existence. When we create and manifest through the crown chakra, utilising the higher mind, creativity expresses itself, giving us the freedom to manifest in the highest form.

My healing journey through my higher self and soul essence has inspired me to heal through symbols. I understand that this clearing and healing is my transition from the Piscean Age to the Age of Aquarius. I have noticed that a lot of souls that incarnate at this moment in time are clearing not just for their own soul, but for the whole soul group and all of humanity (if it's in that soul's desire). The beliefs and energies of the Piscean Age have no place in the Age of Aquarius, so it is imperative that these are transmuted to help with the ascension process to the higher frequencies and dimensions.

The Healing Vibration of Symbols

I have been guided to draw and use the following symbols, and they now form a major part of my healing, both for myself and for others. The feedback from clients and learners who've used these in their own healings or practices has been of immense shifts and access to more light, resulting in a harmonious transition and an anchoring of the feminine energies within.

The Reforming Form Symbol

The following symbol, (*Figure 18, below*) is shown to me as a frequency of light that transmutes energies from the Piscean Age. Working with this symbol helps clear genetic, ancestral, karmic, soul group, past-present-future, masculine, feminine, physical, mental, emotional, spiritual energies on all realms, planes and dimensions. This is what I affectionately term *'the lot'*.

Figure 18. The Reforming Form symbol

When looked at through numerology, this symbol holds the vibration of the following numbers:

* ✳ **4** representing illumination and initiation, symbolises putting ideas into form.

* ✳ **5** representing the perfect human and also harmony, balance and Divine grace.

* ✳ **12** representing cosmic order.

* ✳ **16** representing karmic energy. When transmuted to the higher vibration it expresses itself as love of humanity and the desire to uplift others in the cause of harmony.

The following technique is a very simple form of healing.

Technique No. 28 Karmic Clearance and Embracing Divine Will and Purpose

➢ Using the **Combined Technique No. 5**, from your core self, ground into Mother Earth, turn your master tap on to release emotions back to the Earth, and surrender thoughts to the higher mind.

➢ Set the intention that you are connecting with your pure soul essence through this stream of consciousness and that you are healing 'the lot'.

➢ Set the intention that you are working from your purest highest light and that you only bring the purest highest form of light into your energy field.

➢ Whilst in this energy, take your awareness to the symbol on page 130.

➢ Imagine yourself stepping into the centre of the symbol, as if you're stepping into a frequency of light.

➢ Imagine you are surrounded by 16 different layers and depths of pure light energy.

➢ Hold your focus on the pure light in the centre of the symbol for a few moments, allowing your energy frequency to meet with the pure high energy frequency of the symbol (remember, this is done through your pure stream of consciousness and pure soul essence).

➢ Imagine the symbol and pure, cosmic light connecting in deeper through your third eye.

➢ Allow your energy to respond to the pure healing light (remember, your lower mind is surrendering to the higher mind, and your chakras are releasing negativity through the taps back to Mother Earth).

➢ Sense this pure energy transmuting negative energies.

➢ From this place of purity and light, set the following intention out loud to the cosmos, 'Under the Laws of Cosmic Light, of All That Is and All That I AM, I unattach myself from all karmic energies and I transmute them to their highest vibration so that I may open my heart centre to the love of humanity and I may commit my will to uplifting myself and others in the cause of harmony. So it is, it is done, so doth it be.'

➢ Stay in this energy for as long as you feel is necessary. When ready, take your awareness back to your core self.

➢ Ground yourself into Mother Earth and give thanks.

Divine Will

Sanaya Roman, through her guide *Orin*, describes Divine will and purpose as having seven qualities. These are: the will to initiate, to unify, to evolve, to harmonise, to act, to cause and to express. When we work in harmony with Mother Earth through our lower chakras, through our true self and through our higher mind and soul essence, we bring ourselves into alignment with our soul purpose and the Divine will. When we use our will for the greatest and highest good of all, we discover that synchronicities in life unfold to take us to where we need to be, opening us up to the opportunities that life has to offer.

This technique is also very useful to do when you feel the need to harmonise with your pure self. It takes you back into alignment and helps you to unattach from whatever problem or issue you have. It also takes you deep within yourself so that you may fully connect and embrace with your highest, purest potential.

The Feminine Symbol

Another symbol I like to work with is the Divine feminine energy symbol. This connects in with beautiful frequencies of cosmic light, which represents the feminine aspect of form and helps us to bring in the higher frequencies of the Aquarian age.

Figure 19. The Feminine symbol

The Age of Aquarius is unfolding and reawakening in all of humanity the feminine aspect and the goddess energy within. I've been personally working on strengthening this connection. The more I clear the Piscean energies, the easier it is to access the feminine energies. It's about finding the balance. The following symbol has a depth and a softness to it, which means that when working with the frequencies of cosmic light that it represents, it helps shift vibrations and takes you into alignment under the Laws of Cosmic Light so that you may fully embrace what the Age of Aquarius needs to unfold in you.

Technique No. 29 Connecting with Inner Divine Feminine Energy

> Using the **Combined Technique No. 5,** from your core self, ground into Mother Earth, turn your master tap on to release emotions back to the Earth, and surrender thoughts to the higher mind.

> Set the intention that you are connecting with your pure soul essence through this stream of consciousness and that you are healing 'the lot'.

> Set the intention that you are working from your purest, highest light and that you only bring the purest, highest form of light into your energy field.

> Whilst in this energy, take your awareness to the symbol on page 133.

> Imagine yourself stepping into the centre of the symbol, as if you're stepping into a frequency of light.

> Imagine you are held and embraced in soft layers of pure light energy.

> Hold your focus on the pure light in the centre of the symbol for a few moments, allowing your energy frequency to meet with the pure, high energy frequency of the symbol (remember

that this is done through your pure stream of consciousness and pure soul essence).

➢ Imagine the symbol and pure cosmic light connecting in deeper through your third eye.

➢ Allow your energy to respond to the pure, healing light (remember, your lower mind is surrendering to the higher mind, and your chakras are releasing negativity through the taps back to Mother Earth).

➢ Sense this pure energy nurturing your energies and replenishing your light.

➢ From this place of purity and light set the following intention out loud to the cosmos: *'Under the Laws of Cosmic Light, of All That Is and All That I AM, I intend here and now to commit my will to nurturing in myself and others peace and goodwill for all mankind. I reawaken cellular memories of Divine feminine nurturing love and compassion for myself and all of humanity. So it is, it is done, so doth it be.'*

➢ Imagine your higher mind working with you as you reach up and bring your higher mind down into your lower mind.

➢ Let it settle into a natural state of comfort and fit.

➢ Allow your higher mind to download this light of peace and goodwill into your lower mind.

➢ Get a sense of your mind filling with this light, and fully embrace it into your mind.

➢ Allow this light to extend down into your heart centre.

➢ Sense your heart centre opening to receive this nurturing, feminine light of peace and goodwill, and fully embrace it into your heart centre.

➢ Sense your heart centre opening fully in peace and goodwill.

➢ Allow this light to extend down into your gut, and fully embrace it into your core.

➤ From this place, imagine your willpower stepping into this Divine, feminine, nurturing love and compassion.

➤ State out loud the following intention: *'Under the Laws of Cosmic light, of All That Is and All That I AM, I commit my will to do God's will in line with my soul purpose and the Divine plan. I intend to re-awaken every cell of my feminine energy of power and light and nurturing love. I fully embrace this powerful energy of my soul, and I ground it into my connection with Mother Earth. I intend that I am in full alignment as a 'human' 'being' of light, power and love. I am filled with compassion and the mindset of the Aquarian Age of service to and love for all of humanity. I do this for the greatest and highest good of all concerned. So it is, it is done, so doth it be.'*

➤ Take as long as this healing needs and sense the cells of your body re-awaken to this energy.

➤ When ready, take your awareness back to your core self.

➤ Ground yourself into Mother Earth and give thanks.

Light Bearers

The use of the above techniques and the clearing of the energies enables us to access and bring in more light, taking us from our previous role as light workers to that of light bearers. It is also my understanding that as we are one with all, we can access and bring light into all areas of our existence. Therefore, working on the soul group level has far more impact in assisting souls in this transition from one age to the next.

It's very important that we realise that on a soul group level we are all one and that we are at one with each other. There are numerous books in print that help us to understand how and why we incarnate in our soul group, the lessons and growth we offer each other, as well as the numerous contracts our souls have for growth in this lifetime. Sanaya Roman, Caroline Myss, David Furlong and Gary Zukav have written beautifully on these topics, and I greatly respect these authors.

The Triangular Symbol

The following symbol brings with it a cosmic frequency of light that allows your healing to extend to that of the soul group. This symbol carries cosmic frequencies of light into the mindset of the soul group, so that those souls wishing to avail themselves of the healing may do so on a multidimensional level, assisting the whole soul group on their ascension.

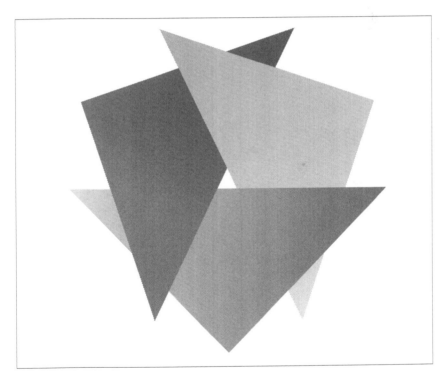

Figure 20. The Triangular symbol

Technique No. 30 Embracing the Mindset of Divine Wisdom and Light

➤ Using the **Combined Technique No. 5,** from your core self, ground into Mother Earth, turn your master tap on to release emotions back to the Earth, and surrender thoughts to the higher mind.

➤ Set the intention that you are connecting with your pure soul essence through this stream of consciousness and that you are healing 'the lot'.

➤ Set the intention that you are working from your purest, highest light and that you only bring the purest, highest form of light into your energy field.

➤ Whilst in this energy, take your awareness to the coloured triangular symbol above.

➤ Imagine yourself stepping into the triangular shape at the centre of the symbol, as if you're stepping into a frequency of light.

➤ Allow the symbol to support the energies of your core self (remember, this is done through your pure stream of consciousness and your pure soul essence).

➤ Imagine your core self totally unattached to all other energies.

➤ Imagine the coloured triangular symbol and pure cosmic light connecting in deeper through your third eye.

➤ Allow your energy to respond to the pure healing light (remember, your lower mind is surrendering to the higher mind, and your chakras are releasing negativity through the taps back to Mother Earth).

➤ From this place of purity and light, set the following intention out loud to the cosmos: *'Under the Laws of Cosmic Light, of All That Is and All That I AM, I intend that I surrender all negative thinking, patterns of thought and mindsets that are no longer in alignment with my higher self and my soul purpose in line with the Divine plan. I fully embrace the mindset of Divine wisdom and light. I open this healing up to the whole soul group and ask that all souls wishing to avail of this healing may do so, for the greatest and highest good of all concerned, so it is, it is done, so doth it be.'*

➤ Sense this pure energy dismantling patterns in the conscious and subconscious mind.

➤ Imagine your higher mind working with you as you reach up and bring your higher mind down into your lower mind.

➤ Let it settle into a natural state of comfort and fit.

➤ Allow your higher mind to download the mindset of Divine wisdom and light.

➤ Get a sense of your mind filling with this light, and fully embrace it into your mind.

➤ Allow this light to extend down into your heart centre.

➤ Sense your heart centre opening to receive this Divine Light and fully embrace it into your heart centre.

➤ Sense your heart centre opening fully in wisdom and light.

➤ Allow this light to extend down into your gut, and fully embrace it into your core.

➤ From this place, imagine your willpower stepping into this Divine wisdom and light.

➤ State out loud the following intention: *'Under the Laws of Cosmic Light, of All That Is and All That I AM, I stand in my power and light and I set the intention that I am on my path of ascension, bringing Divine wisdom and light into my entire existence, 'the lot'. I open this healing to the whole soul group, to those souls wishing to avail of this healing, so that we may transcend and be in alignment with our Divine connection to Source and ascend as a whole soul group at one with all that is. So it is, it is done, so doth it be.'*

- ➢ Take as long as this healing needs and sense the cells of your body re-awaken to this energy.
- ➢ When ready, take your awareness back to your core self.
- ➢ Ground yourself into Mother Earth and give thanks.

The Spiral Symbol

For me, this symbol is the culmination of everything mentioned in this book. This symbol acts as a two-way channel, carrying cosmic light through the levels, layers and planes of existence down through our soul, our higher mind and into our energy fields. It also communicates our intentions through the higher mind, the soul group, the over soul, the masters, guides, angels and teachers - right through to Source. This symbol draws together the energies of all the symbols into one form of wholeness and completeness, and it acts as a recalibration of your core-self signature, realigning and re-harmonising on every level of your existence, bringing you into alignment in the *now*.

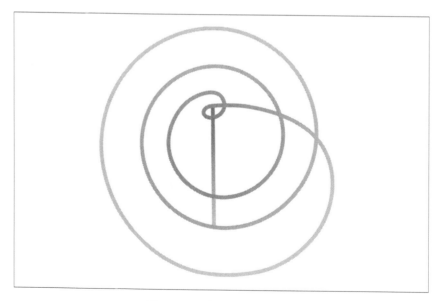

Figure 21. The Spiral symbol

Technique No. 31 Channelling Light Through the Planes of Existence

> Using the **Combined Technique No. 5**, from your core self, ground into Mother Earth, turn your master tap on to release emotions back to the Earth, and surrender thoughts to the higher mind.

> Set the intention that you are connecting with your pure soul essence through this stream of consciousness and that you are healing 'the lot'.

> Set the intention that you are working from your purest, highest light and that you only bring the purest, highest form of light into your energy field.

> Whilst in this energy, take your awareness to the spiral symbol above.

> Imagine yourself stepping into the light at the centre of the symbol, as if you're stepping into a frequency of light.

> Allow your frequency to resonate with the frequency of the symbol.

> Get a sense of your energy centres being fully aligned with your core self and light.

> Get a sense of your vastness of light.

> Imagine the spiral symbol and pure cosmic light connecting in deeper through your third eye.

> Imagine you can sense the expansiveness of your soul power.

> Imagine this expansiveness of soul power and light fully aligning your core self with the highest frequencies and higher dimensions of Mother Earth.

> Allow your energy to respond to the pure, healing light (remember, your lower mind is surrendering to the higher mind, and your chakras are releasing negativity through the taps back to Mother Earth).

➤ From this place of purity and light, set the following intention out loud to the cosmos: *'Under the Laws of Cosmic Light, of All That Is and All That I AM, I set the intention now that I am whole, I am complete, I am a perfect human being, I am in harmony with Divine grace, and I am the perfect form through cosmic order according to the laws. And, in this place of perfect being, I transmute to my higher power and this higher power I bring into form through cosmic light. So it is, it is done, so doth it be.'*

➤ Allow your higher mind to download the mindset of higher power.

➤ Get a sense of your mind filling with this light and fully embrace it into your mind.

➤ Allow this light to extend down into your heart centre.

➤ Sense your heart centre opening to receive this higher power and fully embrace it into your heart centre.

➤ Sense your heart centre opening fully in higher power.

➤ Allow this light to extend down into your gut, and fully embrace it into your core.

➤ From this place, imagine your willpower stepping into higher power.

➤ State out loud the following intention: *'I stand in my power and light and I set the intention that I bring my human form and existence into my higher power of Divine Light, that I may fully embrace the higher frequencies of light. So it is, it is done, so doth it be.'*

➤ Take as long as this healing needs and sense yourself embracing this higher frequency of light.

➤ When ready, take your awareness back to your core self.

➤ Ground yourself into Mother Earth and give thanks.

Technique No. 32 Grounded in the Now

In order to follow through on intentions, it's important that these, as well as our focus and will, are in full alignment with each other. To achieve this we need to be in the *now*.

This is a very powerful technique and instantly impacts on the auric field. When I use this technique with learners and get them to scan each other's auras before and after, the results are amazing - it's as if the person disconnects from everything around them, leaving them unattached and totally in the now.

➢ Using the **Combined Technique No. 5**, from your core self, ground into Mother Earth, turn your master tap on to release emotions back to the Earth, and surrender thoughts to the higher mind.

➢ Set the intention that you are connecting with your pure soul essence and healing 'the lot'.

➢ Set the intention that you reach up to your higher mind and download the mindset of *grounded in the now*.

➢ Imagine this mindset downloading into your lower mind.

➢ Imagine the Reforming Form symbol, the Feminine symbol, the Triangular symbol and the Spiral symbol and imagine placing these symbols in the mindset of *grounded in the now*.

➢ Imagine these symbols creating a vibrational frequency, a pattern of light in the mindset.

➢ State out loud: *'Under the Laws of Cosmic Light, of All That Is and All That I AM, I intend here and now to fully download the mindset of **being in the now**, of **being safe in the now**, of **trusting in the now**, of **being happy in the now**, of **being grounded in the now**. I surrender to my higher mind any mindset that contradicts these statements and intentions. I set the intention that my thoughts default to **being grounded in the now**. So it is, it is done, so doth it be.'*

➤ Extend this pattern of light from the mind down into the heart centre.

➤ Imagine all four symbols in the pattern of *grounded in the now* in the heart centre.

➤ Imagine these symbols contributing towards the vibrational frequency in the heart centre, influencing the pattern of light.

➤ Set the intention that you fully embrace this energy deep within your heart centre, whilst stating out loud: *'I surrender to Mother Earth all emotions that contradict these statements and intentions. I set the intention that all emotions are **grounded in the now**. So it is, it is done, so doth it be.'*

➤ Extend this pattern of light from the heart centre down into your core. Now extend it through your solar plexus, your sacral and your base chakras.

➤ Imagine all four symbols, in the pattern of *grounded in the now,* creating a vibrational frequency in each of the lower chakras. This creates a pattern of light.

➤ Set the intention that you fully embrace this energy deep within your core, whilst stating out loud: *'I surrender to Mother Earth all energies that contradict these statements and intentions. I intend that my energies are **grounded in the now**. So it is, it is done, so doth it be.'*

➤ Imagine your ego and your willpower stepping into this frequency of *grounded in the now.*

➤ State out loud: 'I surrender my ego and my willpower, 'the lot', to this frequency of grounded in the now, and I ground this down into Mother Earth. So it is, it is done, so doth it be.

➤ Imagine this frequency, this pattern of light, extending down into your connection with Mother Earth.

    o   Imagine all four symbols being placed into your connection with Mother Earth, through the genetic, ancestral, karmic, soul group, past lives and epigenetic links.

Once you have completed this technique, the quick imagery and the affirmation, *'I am grounded in the now'* will take your energy there instantly.

Conclusion

Through the research-based evidence presented in this book, we can conclude that we are human beings emerging from Mother Earth into the energy patterns of all that's gone before us. Our choices and decisions in this life are influenced by our ancestors' beliefs, habits, attitudes and life experiences. We are further influenced by the planets and their ongoing shifts. Our human structures are built on the protein blocks of life and are fuelled by the foods we eat and the chemical legacy we are born into.

Modern research and the amazing doctors and scientists who are willing to look beyond the limitations of Newtonian science (authors such as those are mentioned in this book) are helping us to expand our understanding of life as human beings beyond the limitations of the left brain. These authors have opened our thinking and supported the expansion of our minds to the awareness that we can, and do, influence our reality. This is how I see our free will vs destiny. It's what we *do* with what we've *been given* that's important. We are powerful beings and through positive intent and purpose we can change our energy and heal right down to the cellular level.

Whilst we can't change the past, we can change the energy imprints, the beliefs, the patterns, the habits and the attitudes. We need to stop seeing ourselves as victims of the past and instead view ourselves as builders of the future. We can create what we so desire and we can set new patterns of change to help form a positive, loving, peaceful, joyous new life, new Earth and new future.

This is the legacy I want to pass on to future generations. And, for those of you who do believe in reincarnation, this is the legacy I wish to return to if I do have a future life ahead of me!

It is also my belief that souls incarnated at this moment in time are souls who have agreed to - or who are willing to - bring about much needed change. Astrologers have predicted that these times will involve great shifts and expansion. Some of us have woken up to our soul's yearning for change and more and more souls are looking for a meaning to life, a desire driven from deep within.

These **Infusion Techniques** are self-empowerment techniques designed to help you create your own reality, based on higher mind thinking and grounding the past into the now. We heal not just ourselves but also Mother Earth.

Techniques Developed Through This Book

By now you should have developed the techniques to enable you to:

✓ Connect with your core self and remain self-centred within your auric field.

✓ Remain grounded in the now unattached to other people's emotional dramas.

✓ Have a healthy grounding with Mother Earth.

✓ Work through your higher mind.

✓ Open to your insight and wisdom.

✓ Understand the importance of releasing emotional ties and binds.

✓ Open your heart centre to unconditional love and trust.

✓ Become empowered in your whole, true self.

✓ Gain true self-control.

✓ Forgive the past and let go with ease.

✓ Develop a loving, respectful acceptance and tolerance for yourself and others.

✓ Heal on a soul and soul group level.

Further Development & Frequently Asked Questions

I understand that you may have questions in relation to your experiences of working with these techniques. A Frequently Asked Questions section is available on my website: ***www.holisticenergy.co.uk.***

Should you wish to continue your healing journey using these and similar techniques, I have developed *online training courses* to help you:

- ✓ Connect with your core
- ✓ Experience your true self-healing power and wisdom
- ✓ Work through your higher mind
- ✓ Access your innate inner guidance for a smoother life experience
- ✓ Align ego energies with your soul essence
- ✓ Truly fulfil your soul purpose in line with the Divine plan
- ✓ Ground your past/present/future into the now
- ✓ Become the true master of the self

Step into your power and take control of your destiny - go to www.holisticenergy.co.uk and sign up now.

Wishing you much love and healing light,

Acknowledgements

I would like to pay special thanks to;

Philip Kidson for encouraging the writing of this book and for his immense support along the way.

Charmaine Faulds, Phil Ryan, Claire Edmondson and *Agata Rerutko* for taking the time to work through all 32 techniques.

Justin Smith for taking my images to a creative level.

Jo Austwick for putting my ideas into art form.

Najwa Ezzaher for supporting the MP3 recordings of the techniques in this book.

Frazer Green Photography for the back cover potrait.

Danielle Wrate of Wrate's Editing Services (www.wrateseditingservices.co.uk) for helping to make this book happen.

To all my clients and learners, who over the years have helped me to develop and grow.

And a very special thanks to you, *the reader*, for reading this book.

'We are all souls on a journey of expression and expansiveness, offering each other solace and hope when and where it's needed.'

Bibliography

Axe, Josh. *Eat Dirt*. Print.

Davies, Brenda. *Journey Of The Soul*. London: Hodder Mobius, 2003. Print.

Dispenza, Joe. *Evolve Your Brain*. Dearfield, FL: Health Communications, 2007. Print.

Furlong, David. *Healing Your Ancestral Patterns*, 2014. Print.

Hamilton. David R and David R Hamilton. *Is Your Life Mapped Out?* London: Hay House, 2012. Print.

Hay, Louise. *Mirror Work*. [Place of publication not identified]: Hay House UK Ltd, 2016. Print.

Hay, Louise L. *You Can Heal Your Life*. Carlsbad, Calif.: Hay House, 2004. Print.

Leaf, Caroline. *Switch On Your Brain*. Print.

Lipton, Bruce H. *The Biology Of Belief*, Santa Rosa, CA; Mountain of Love/Elite Books, 2005. Print.

McTaggart, Lynne. *The Field*. New York: Harper, 2008. Print.

McTaggart, Lynne. *The Intention Experiment*. New York: Free Press, 2007. Print.

Myss, Caroline M. *Sacred Contracts*. New York: Harmony Books, 2001. Print.

Noontil, Annette. *The Body Is The Barometer Of The Soul So Be Your Own Doctor II*. East Burwood, Vic.: Annette Noontil, 1994. Print.

Orin, and Sanaya Roman. *Soul Love*. Tiburon, Calif.: H.J. Kramer, 1997. Print.

Pert, Candace B. *Molecules Of Emotion*. New York, NY: Scribner, 1997. Print.

Roberts, M. *Tissue Salts For Healthy Living*. South Africa: New Africa Books (Pty), 2003. Print.

Taylor, Jill Bolte. *My Stroke Of Insight*. New York: Viking, 2008. Print.

Zukav, Gary. *The Seat Of The Soul*. Print.

Astrology websites

Kaypacha - http://newparadigmastrology.com/

Alan Oken - http://www.alanoken.com/

Rick Levine - https://www.youtube.com/watch?v=HlKzi1ZVVGE

18283107R00091

Printed in Great Britain
by Amazon